M000086736

Legal Terminology

An Historical Guide to the Technical Language of Law

Legal Terminology

An Historical Guide to the Technical Language of Law

Daniel Williman

broadview press

Canadian Cataloguing in Publication Data

Williman, Daniel
  Legal terminology

Bibliography: p.
Includes index.
ISBN 0-921149-02-6

1. Law- Terms and phrases.   2. Law- History and
criticism.   I. Title

K50.W55 1986   340'.03   C86-095046-8

broadview press   in the U.S.: broadview press
P.O. Box 1243   421 Center St.
Peterborough, Canada, K9J 7H5   Lewiston, N.Y. 14092

Printed and bound in Canada by
Gagné Ltd.

Cover design by Falcom Design & Communications

Cover illustration: adapted from
the frontspiece of *Ignoramus* (see p. 90).

Contents

for Laurel Nilsen

Preface

As a student at the Pontifical Institute of Mediaeval Studies in Toronto some eighteen years ago, I enjoyed noting the antique flavor of the language of Ontario's lawyers and courts, a daily echo of the old legal systems that formed the content of the courses I was then taking in Roman Civil Law, Canon Law, and English Common Law. Later, as a teacher and researcher in the Latin tradition of European civilization, I have frequently been asked the "real" meaning of some legal Latin word or phrase, and been forced to admit that, since only lawyers used such little antiques any more, the technical legal meaning was the most real meaning. Nevertheless, the surviving fragments of departed legal systems, like pieces of pottery that turn up in a building excavation, are worth careful study by a classicist and historian. They provide evidence of a continuous 900-year-old legal tradition, some of whose roots go back twice that far and more. The language can help to uncover legal history, and the historical study can illuminate contemporary law.

The SUNY-Binghamton course in Legal Terminology had its first run in the Fall semester of 1981, with the encouragement of Emilio Roma, director of the Law and Society Program, and Anthony Preus, chair of the Department of Classical and Near Eastern Studies. A Vice-President's Curriculum Development Grant fostered the early research. Dr. Martha Jean Schecter, Member of the Bar of Kentucky and of New York, combed the vocabulary to eliminate words and phrases that are no longer in current use, and made important corrections to many entries. Ms. Lovette George helped to winnow the list further. The contents have since been replanned and amplified. For their reading of the text and suggestions for its improvement I am grateful to Bert Hansen, Gerald Kadish, and Michael Mittelstadt, and the students of Classics 113 in 1981, 1982, 1983 and 1986.

Introduction

This book is about the technical language of Anglo-American law. It looks for the sources of that technical language in European legal systems of the past, and tries to see the language and the history each in the light of the other. Care has been taken to make the book readable and accurate, and every technical word, phrase and maxim has been listed in the index, in hopes of serving readers who will wish to use the book for their own pleasure and enlightenment as a discursive sketch of legal antiquities or as a reference tool.

The selection of legal terminology presented here is far too meager to lay claim to being a legal dictionary. There are fewer than 900 items, counting words, phrases and maxims. I have tried to limit the word list to language that 1) occurs in current usage and that 2) has links, especially French and Latin links, to medieval and ancient law. For current legal usage, *Black's Law Dictionary* is recommended. The etymology of borrowed and naturalized English terms should be pursued in the *Oxford English Dictionary,* and classical Latin background in the *Oxford Latin Dictionary.* Similarly, the sketches of earlier legal systems which are presented here do not amount to a history of law; for that reason, each historical chapter is accompanied by a short supplementary bibliography.

Finally, this book makes no contribution to the sociolinguistic,

philosophical and ethical questions raised by the jargon called
Legalese, or the impact of obsolete language on legislation and
legal communication, or the debate over clarity and precision. For
these matters, the definitive survey is David Mellinkoff, *The
Language of the Law*. Further explorations in social linguistics
are found in Shirley Brice Heath, "The Context of Professional
Languages: an Historical Overview" in *Language in Public Life*
(1979), pp. 102-118; and William M. O'Barr, "The Language of
the Law" in *Language in the USA* (1981) pp. 386-406. The eloquent
and useful guide by Henry Weihofen, *Legal Writing Style* (1961)
gives solid practical advice and good remedies for pathological
Legalese.

Chapter One

Language and European History

At the beginning it should be useful to define the subject of the book and to identify its place within the large complex of the sciences of language. This book is about etymology, the history of the meanings of words. Linguistics and grammar have something to contribute to this investigation, but they are not essential to it. Not the whole English vocabulary but only one technical sub-vocabulary, legal terminology, is under consideration here. The method of investigation is historical rather than analytical.

Ordinary spoken English has borrowed thousands of words and word-elements from Latin and French. The technical vocabularies of scientific English are full of terminology adopted from Greek and Latin. It is possible, therefore, to *analyze* the foreign components of general English, or the technical language of the physical sciences, and use that analysis for further understanding and vocabulary-building. For example, the Latin prefix *sub* appears in hundreds of words, such as **suffer, subordinate,** and **support,** always with a meaning related to its Latin meaning, "under". There are four Greek word-elements in the word **electroencephalogram** which add up to its meaning, "an electronic map of the brain". These are demonstrations of analytical etymology.

The language of Anglo-American law confronts the student with a very different sort of problem. The law is a partially self-contained culture within the general one. Most of the time, lawyers

speak ordinary English, but 1) they have special meanings for many
words, and 2) they have a special, professional memory of other
words and phrases from Latin, French, and old-fashioned English,
that come from earlier stages of the study and practice of the law.
A general analysis does not get us far toward understanding this
professional dialect; it only shows us that most of the foreign
elements were originally Latin and that most of these passed
through French into the lawyers' English. Beyond that, each word
or phrase must be examined for its own individual history *within
the tradition of the law.* Some grand movements in the history
of language must be understood, however, because they set the
general context for our study of specifically legal English.

Some Indo-European Languages

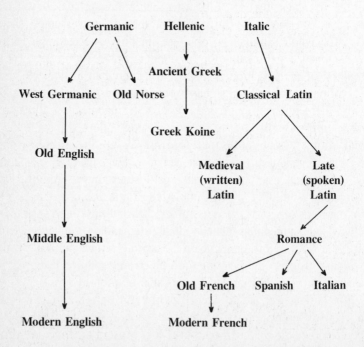

The table above shows the family relations of the various languages that appear in the study of English legal terminology. Each arrow in this (very selective) table indicates the passage of time and the changing of a language, under constant use by large numbers of speakers and writers, into a noticeably different language. Latin, the language of the ancient city of Rome and its empire, became the language of all of Italy and of Gaul (modern France) as the empire expanded. When the empire collapsed, beginning in the 4th century AD, the intercommunication between its regions, which had kept their language more or less unified, became rare. Late Latin or Primitive Romance was spoken more and more differently in the different countries of Western Europe. In the course of fifteen hundred years, Romance divided into different modern languages including the two that we know as Italian and French. Both are descended from Latin, and their vocabularies are mostly derived directly from Latin. For example, the Italian *giudice* and the French *juge* are both derived from the Latin *judex* and mean the same thing: judge.

English, as the table clearly shows, belongs to an entirely different branch, the Germanic branch, of the Indo-European language family. English is not descended from Greek or Latin, much less from French. Why, then, does it contain so much vocabulary material from those languages? And in particular, why does its specialized legal terminology come mostly from Latin and French?

English culture and the English language have inhabited the same home island of Great Britain since the Anglo-Saxons invaded it from the continent in the 4th century AD. There has been only one military conquest of the island since then — the invasion of the Normans under William the Conqueror in 1066, which gave England a French-speaking ruling class. The Normans then monopolized warfare, the land, the land law and the courts, in French, for three centuries.

In a sense, England succumbed to two more purely linguistic invasions. Through the whole Middle Ages in Europe and England, roughly from 500 to 1500 AD, the Christian Church and its clergy held a near monopoly of literacy and book-learning, including legal

records and legal scholarship, all in Latin. And Greek made its
mark on all the European cultures because it was the original
language of the New Testament, as well as of western mathematics,
logic and technical grammar, philosophy, medicine, and the natural
sciences.

So it happens that the English language, due to the domination
of England by a Norman military aristocracy, and centuries of
respect for religious authority and professional expertise, now has
a vocabulary which is *mostly* borrowed from French, Latin, and
Greek. England's Law Latin is a fragment of Medieval Latin; and
Law French is Old French as it was spoken in the law courts of
England.

Respect for authority is a strong element in Anglo-American
culture. At its best, this respect is what causes us to give generous
recognition and rewards for excellent achievement in the arts and
sciences, regardless of the family background and personal style
of the achiever. At its worst, it is silly snobbery. In between, in
daily life we tend to assume that what we are told by the doctor,
the minister of religion, and the legal specialist is true and worthy
of respect. If their language is somewhat difficult to understand,
we normally do not resent this; in fact we expect high sophistica-
tion to sound sophisticated. When we acquire a little or a lot of
professional knowledge, we use the professional terminology to
express it. On their side, the learned professionals are accustomed
to learning their craft, then discussing and practising it, in a
language that they share fully only with their fellow professionals.
They do not object to sounding like doctors, priests, lawyers; instead, they enjoy the spontaneous respect it brings them from the
rest of society. Furthermore, they use their technical language as
a professional dialect — "jargon" is the pejorative term — that
unifies the members of the professional group and excludes
outsiders.

It would be useful at this point to distinguish three levels of recep-
tion of foreign words into a language (English in the present case):
borrowing, adoption, and derivation.

1) **Borrowed** words are picked up from other languages by some

English speakers for the sake of their usefulness but they are not changed in their forms (except by mistake), and they do not become truly English words, that is, part of the general vocabulary of the language. The Latin *mens rea* and the French *feme covert* are examples of borrowings.

2) **Adopted** words have become English words, but with little or no change in form, like the formerly Latin *per diem* or *alibi*, or the formerly French *demurrer*.

3) English **derivatives** may have come into the language by adoption, but over time they have changed form to look and sound more English, for example *jail* (older English spelling *gaol*) came from the Latin *caveola*, "little hole"; *judge* and *jury* are from the French *juge* and *juree*.

Terminology

There are nearly one thousand terms and maxims under consideration in this book, distributed among the following chapters. Chapters 1 and 2 are about language and legal history in general. Chapters 4, 7, 10, 14 and 19 deal with the history of law, concentrating on the legal systems of the past that have provided terms for our legal language. The other chapters explain a sampling of the terminology of particular legal topics such as Real Property and Torts. It will be obvious that many of the terms could just as well have appeared under different headings, and I do not mean to imply that "sua sponte", for instance, is exclusively associated with procedure because it appears in the Pleading and Trial word list.

The word lists in this book are not intended to substitute for a dictionary. While I have attempted to include only words that are in current use, the explanations that are given here concentrate on origins and traditions rather than modern usage. For an up-to-date technical understanding of any word, a legal dictionary such as Black's or Ballentine's must be consulted, and for more linguistic and etymological information, the Oxford English Dictionary.

These symbols are used in brackets to explain the linguistic history of a word:

>	translated to
A	Arabic
E	English
F	French
G	Germanic in general
H	Hellenic, i.e. Greek
I	Italian
L	Latin
N	Old Norse

For example, the entry *habendum* [GE > L] indicates a Latin word which entered the legal vocabulary as a translation of the Germanic and English phrase "to have" [and to hold]; *cede* [LFE] was once the Latin *cedere* and later the French *ceder*.

Quotation marks indicate a translation or other re-rendering of the word or phrase, a replacement definition. The following abbreviated Latin notes are used with their customary meanings:

cf.	=	*confer,* "compare"
e.g.	=	*exempli gratia,* "for example"
i.e.	=	*id est,* "that is"
q.v.	=	*quod vide,* "and see that"

A suggestion is in order about the pronunciation of the foreign-language terms. French has its own proper standards of pronunciation, and Latin has more than one: a classical pronunciation and a medieval (alias the ecclesiastical or Italianate) pronunciation. In a way, it might be more correct to pronounce legal Latin according to those rules, and some lawyers do so. But it is more common — and therefore correct — to speak technical legal French and Latin words, especially the latter, as if they were English,

LANGUAGE AND EUROPEAN HISTORY

e.g. "fiery fayshes" for *fieri facias*. Current pronunciation by lawyers should be followed, and *Black's Law Dictionary* shows what that is. When in doubt, speak boldly.

Until this century, lawyers were expected to have been educated in the Liberal Arts, including Latin grammar, and the Latin fragments which survive in technical legal language are grammatically correct Latin. A user who does not understand Latin grammar should refrain from tampering with them unassisted, since a single letter changed can alter the grammar and change or empty the meaning of the word. Even commonplace rules can fail: the familiar plural of *datum* is *data,* and so *forum* has the plural *fora*; on the model *alumnus — alumni,* several guilty men are *rei.* But *corpus* is a neuter from a different group, and its plural is *corpora; onus* has the plural *onera.* The noun *actus* is masculine, but its plural is also *actus*; similarly, *prospectus — prospectus.* But there is also an adjective *actus*, which appears in the phrase *res inter alios acta,* whose plural would be *res . . . actae.* The correct plurals *actus rei, mentes reae, corpora delicti* or (when several crimes are meant) *corpora delictorum* do not come naturally to a non-Latinist. The reflexive *se* and its adjective forms including *sua* signify masculine, feminine, and plural persons without change of form. In the word lists of this book, Latin plurals are given where they might be useful. *Caveant emptores.*

Chapter Two

The History of Law and Terminology

When our contemporary lawyers talk about law, a large part of their peculiarly legal vocabulary consists of Old French, antique English, and Latin words and phrases. These are a part of their professional heritage from a tradition of the science and practice of law that goes back to the Roman republic, four centuries BC, and that has other roots in the medieval Germanic nations of Europe.

Our Legal Tradition in Brief

One good way to begin a systematic study of legal words and phrases is with a general understanding of the legal systems of the past in which they were generated. The purpose of this book is to explain the terminology historically, and *vice versa,* to illustrate the legal history with the terminology. The chapters that follow are a mixture of historical sketches and topical surveys of the language. Here is a short summary history of the legal traditions, keyed to the diagram on page 16.

Ancient Roman Civil Law became known throughout Europe in the form of the Emperor Justinian's 6th-century *Corpus Juris Civilis,* but not until five centuries after the *Corpus* was compiled. This massive, complete written legal system was recovered late in the 11th century and put to use as 1) the law of the German Holy Roman Empire, which considered itself the successor of the ancient Roman Empire; 2) the law used and enforced by cities and states in much of the old Roman-Law territories, especially in Italy and southern France; and 3) the graduate course in legal theory taught in the medieval universities, including the English ones, which came into being in the 12th century.

The law of the western Christian Church, which developed in Latin, within the Roman Empire and under the influence of Roman Law, was codified beginning in the middle of the 12th century. This "Canon Law" applied to church people and church cases in England as everywhere else in western Europe. For convenient handling of interstate cases and mercantile law, Civil and Canon Law were blended into a judges' common law, the Romano-Canonical *jus commune*.

The Germanic tribes and nations had their several customary laws, unwritten but memorized and woven into the German languages, including Anglo-Saxon. One federation of German tribes, called the Franks (or "Free Men") after they had invaded Roman Gaul in the 3rd century, adopted the local Romance language but maintained their German customary laws. The land and language then took the names France and French, after the Frankish invaders. In the 9th century the Scandinavian Northmen or Normans, also Germanic peoples, invaded the northwest corner of France, which is still called Normandy after them, and repeated the same translation process. When the Normans invaded England in 1066, they brought their customary law with them (in French), and this continued as the law of their class privilege, feudal law.

Beginning in the 12th century the Norman kings of England worked to centralize the laws of the island under their control, but without homogenizing them. England kept a national law of many systems and three languages: the Old English of the majority of the population, the Norman French of the dominant class, and the Latin of the literate clergy. The kings' justice, applied in common throughout the realm, was the English Common Law. At its beginning, this system dealt with only a few questions of

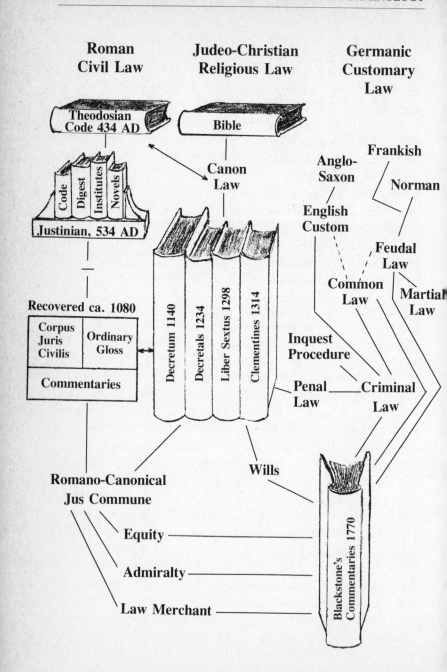

private land law and a few criminal matters.

Amplified by Statutes and supplemented by courts of equity such as Chancery and Admiralty, the Common Law developed into a true national law, although it was not represented in University studies until 1758, when William Blackstone took the Vinerian Chair at Oxford and began the lectures which he published in 1765-1770 as his *Commentaries on the Laws of England.* This first general textbook included and explained the law's linguistic oddities. English speaking Canada was a legal outpost of Great Britain, subject to the legislation of Parliament at Westminster and observing the precedents of the British courts. The United States too, although they were free after the Revolution to choose their own laws from any of a half-dozen sources, gravitated toward the law as found in a few English books, especially Blackstone, and so the British legal tradition, as represented by Blackstone, became the major original source of North American law and of almost all its foreign-language terminology.

Chapter Three

Litigation, Pleading and Trial

The law is strongly conservative in some ways, and the ritual of the courtroom is a notable example. The trial space and its traditional arrangement and furniture contribute to the sense of a special, even a sacred or magic event. The judge's bench, elevated on its tribunal over the verbal fight that takes place in the well of the court; the jury in its box, enclosed and safe from tampering; the public seats outside the bar — these are all liturgical traditions we have inherited from what might be called English architectural procedure. We would still have the prisoner standing in the dock, if we were not so sensitive about dramatizing the presumption of innocence. The orderly sequence of trial is part of "due process", but it is also part of the ritual, traditional character of justice at work. In fact, according to an older idea, "due process" was "due" or "owed" not so much to the weaker party as to the dignity of the law and the court. Even in a democracy, we like our formal justice to look regal and divinely detached. In the dictum of Lord Hewart in **R. v. Sussex Justices** *(King's Bench Reports* 1924, vol. 1, p. 259), "Justice should not only be done, but should manifestly and undoubtedly be seen to be done"; and we want it to look like justice, solidly traditional, even antique.

We want it to sound like justice too, with formal English prose in the pleadings and with atavistic cries and traditional formulaic proclamations like "Oyez! Oyez!" and "God save the United States of America and this honorable court!" The terminology associated with judicial procedure is highly traditional, harking back to the English courts of the long age when their spoken language was French and their record was usually kept in Latin. In the word list for this chapter, about a third of the entries have a French history, and the only Anglo-Saxon ones, *answer* and *hearing,* were introduced to translate the Latin terms *responsio* and *auditio* because the latter sounded too Civil-Law for the English lawyers' taste.

A great American historian of legal procedure, Robert Wyness Millar, traced 23 terms in his article "The Lineage of Some Procedural Words", *American Bar Association Journal* 25 (1939) 1023-1029. Ten items in the following list, and more later, are marked with citations to Millar. References to Broom in this and later chapters refer to Herbert Broom, *A Selection of Legal Maxims, Classified and Illustrated* (7th American, from the 5th London edition; Philadelphia, 1874).

Terminology

action [LFE] a lawsuit; this is the meaning of the Roman Civil Law term *actio,* brought by the *actor* or plaintiff (Millar, p. 1024).

actionable [LFE] capable of being a cause of a lawsuit.

ad damnum [L] "to the loss", the first words of the paragraph in a complaint that states the value of the loss.

ad hoc [L] "for this", for one purpose only, as an attorney *ad hoc* represents a client only for one action or even for only one hearing. The plural would be *ad haec*.

ad litem [L] "for a lawsuit"; a guardian *ad litem* is not a guardian in general, but only a law guardian.

ad testificandum [L] "for testifying"; one purpose of a writ of *habeas corpus*; one kind of subpoena (cf. *duces tecum* below).

adjourn [LFE] "[put off] to a day"; to postpone a trial, sometimes (illogically) *sine die*, "without a day" to reconvene.

affirmative defense [LE] one that establishes (Latin *ad* + *firmat*) a fact; by contrast, a negative defense disproves the complaint or charge.

allegation [LFE] from the Latin *ad* + *legatio*, "a message": the setting out of facts or claims that one intends to prove.

amicus curiae [L] "friend of the court", characterizing a person, not a party to a lawsuit, who files a brief in the public interest or to help the court serve justice. The feminine *amica curiae* might be used, or the plural *amici curiae*, but not if the phrase is to function as an adjective.

answer [L>E] a "swearing back", from the Old English *andswaru*, to translate the Latin *responsio* (Millar, p. 1026).

Audi alteram partem. "Hear the other side." A Latin maxim explained by Broom (pp. 112-116) principally in criminal procedure: "No man should be condemned unheard". The law must inflict no penalty on one who has not been allowed to answer. Broom quotes Justice Fortescue: "The laws of God and man both give the party an opportunity to make his defense, if he has any." It may be that Fortescue was thinking of the argument, at least as old as Bartolo, that even the Creator gave the first man his day in court with the summons "Where art thou, Adam?" (Gn.3.9).

bar [LFE] from a presumed Late Latin *barra*, a pole used as an an obstruction; an impediment to a contract or to a lawsuit; or the physical boundary that separates the owners' portion of a court, a legislative chamber, or a tavern from the public part.

brief [LFE] "something short": the summary of a case made before or after trial; in England, the summary prepared by the solicitor for a trial attorney, on which is marked the fee that will be paid for pleading it in court. The Latin *breve* was also the term for one of the original writs of Common Law.

cede [LFE] "yield (Latin *cedere*)": to surrender or hand over to another. The form concede is used in reference to a point at issue in an argument.

claim [LFE] "cry (Latin *clamare*)", "complain": to demand a right.

complaint [G>FE] "a cry": the French translation of *Klage,* which is still the German word for an action at law (Millar, p. 1026).

contingent fee [LE,GFE] from the Latin *con + tangens,* "leaning", "depending"; a fee that depends upon the attorney's success, a fee "on speculation" or "on spec".

coram [L] "before the face of" a judge; so a writ of error *coram nobis,* "before Ourselves", brought the case to the Court of King's Bench.

counterclaim [LFE] a claim by the defendant back against (Latin *contra*) the plaintiff; its amount is called the set-off.

court [LFE] not from from Latin *curia,* which it often translates, but from *cohors*: a barnyard, gathering of animals or soldiers, a city ward, its assembly, and finally the formal gathering around the king or before a judge (Millar, p. 1024).

de bene esse, d.b.e. [L] "out of well-being", "for the good it might do": provisional and provisionally permissable, as is a deposition taken before trial, if the witness is dying.

defendant [LFE] the one repelling (Latin *defendens*) an attack.

De minimis non curatex. a Latin maxim well translated by Broom (pp. 142-145) "The law does not concern itself with trifles." For example, there are levels of damages below which courts refuse to hear in first instance or on appeal, and minor casual nuisances, e.g. in water and land use, are simply ignored by the law.

demur [LFE] "dwell (Latin *de* + *morare*)", "abide", "take a stand"; therefore the noun *demurrer*, originally the infinitive of the French verb, means the defense's stand that the plaintiff's allegations do not oblige the defendant to answer (Millar, p. 1027). Cf. *demurrage* in chapter 18.

de novo [L] "newly", "again from the beginning".

deposition [LE] "a setting down (Latin *de* + *positio*)" in writing of testimony for the court.

dilatory [LE] from the Latin *latus*, "broad"; "tending to delay" the course of a trial.

duces tecum [L] "you should bring with you" specific documents or material evidence: one kind of subpoena.

esquire [LFE] "shield-bearer", a noble not yet a knight; so an honorific for any gentleman in England, Canada, and other Commonwealth countries, and for an attorney in the United States.

exception [LE] in Civil procedure, an *exceptio* was an unfulfilled condition necessary to an action, or the defense's allegation that such a condition was unfulfilled; later, any objection intended to bar or delay, by either side against the other; cf. **objection** below (Millar, p. 1027).

ex parte [L] "from a side": refers to a proceeding that involves only one of the parties to a lawsuit.

forum non conveniens [L] "inappropriate court", a reason for which a court may decline to hear a case.

gravamen [L] "heaviness", "burden": the material heart of a complaint.

hearing [L>GE] translates the Latin *auditio*.

in camera [L] often translated "in chambers": before a judge, but in his private room (*camera* usually meant a bedchamber), not in public.

in invitum [L] "[proceedings] upon an unwilling person". The feminine would be *in invitam,* plurals *in invitos* or *in invitas.*

interlocutory [LE] "in the midst of the talking (Latin *inter* + *locutus*)": before the end of a suit.

interrogatory [LE] "questioning between (Latin *inter* + *rogatus*)" parties, for the sake of discovery.

joinder [LFE] from the Latin *jungere,* the French *joindre,* "a coupling together", e.g. the combination of several interests in one lawsuit.

letters rogatory [LFE,LE] a letter from a court "questioning", i.e. containing interrogatories to be answered under the order of another court.

mesne [LFE] "middle", neither first (original) nor last (executory) process.

motion [LE] act of a party to move (Latin *movere*) a suit along toward a conclusion.

ne exeat [L] "lest he depart", a writ forbidding a person to leave the jurisdiction of the court.

nolle prosequi, nol. pros. [L] the declaration by a plaintiff or prosecutor "that he does not wish to pursue" a claim or charge.

nonsuit [LFE] failure of the plaintiff to proceed or to prove a case; a dismissal for that reason; a judge may be said "to nonsuit" a plaintiff.

objection [LE] "the throwing in (Latin *ob* + *jacere*)" of an exception; the modern word for what the Civil Law called an exception.

of course [L>E] translates *de cursu,* "from the ordinary sequence of events"; for example, a writ of course is issued on request, without need for any argument of the merits.

pendente lite [L] "while a lawsuit is pending (hanging)". *Lite pendente* is also found, and the noun phrase *lis pendens.*

petition [LE] "a seeking", in Civil Law the quest for a right such as an inheritance; any prayer for justice addressed to a judicial authority (Millar, p. 1026).

plaintiff [LFE] from the Latin *planctivus,* the French *plaintif,* "the complaining one".

pleading [LFE] from the Latin *planctus,* a persuasive speech; the oral arguments in a case, which is what the French *plaidoyer* still means (Millar, p. 1025).

pro bono publico [L] "for the public good", legal services provided free of charge; sometimes reduced to *pro bono.*

process [LE] "a stepping forward". *Processus* was the late medieval term for a particular lawsuit, while *ordo judiciorum* meant what we call "procedure", the proper manner of conducting various *processus.* See Millar, p. 1023.

pro se [L] "for himself/herself/themselves": not through an attorney or by proxy.

respondent [LE] "answerer" to a bill in equity or to an appeal.

retraxit [L] "he [the plaintiff] withdrew" his claim: a bar to further action.

scire facias [L] "you should let [a party] know", an obsolete writ for processes based on the record.

show cause [L>E] the court's order for a party to appear and give reasons why the court should not take particular actions. Translates the Latin *ostensurus quare.*

sua sponte [L] "by his/her/their own wish", voluntarily.

suit, sue [LFE] from the Latin *secta,* "a following", "a pursuit" (Millar, p. 1024).

toll [LFE] "to lift (Latin *tollere*)": to suspend the running of a specified term, e.g. under a statute of limitations.

traverse [LE] "a crosswise position (Latin *trans* + *versum*)", formally denying a plea in common law.

vacate [LE] from the Latin *vacuum*; "to empty", annul, cancel, e.g. a judgement.

witness [E] In Old English, originally, "knowledge", later "testimony", and eventually "the one who gives testimony".

Chapter Four

History I: Roman Civil Law

A. Civil Law History

The law of the city of Rome, which the Romans called Civil
Law in contrast to the Law of (other) Nations, was already well
developed when its oldest surviving text, the Twelve Tables, was
written down in the middle of the 5th century BC. The law continued to develop as the city republic grew to control of the entire
Mediterranean world. In the last century BC, Rome lost its
republican constitution to an imperial autocracy, and finally (438
AD) experienced the historical humiliation of having an imperial
compilation of the law dictated to the Senate at Rome by the
emperor Theodosius II from his throne in Constantinople (now
Istanbul). The *Theodosian Code* was taken to be the true Roman
Law in Europe as the empire there died out, leaving behind only
memories, stately ruins, the Latin language, and the Roman
Christian Church.

A century after Theodosius II, the emperor Justinian laid plans
to reconquer the European part of the empire from its German
invaders, and as part of his scheme he had the law codified again.
The work was finished in 534 AD, and comprised 1) a complete
Code of laws in force, 2) a book called the *Pandects* or *Digest*
of the opinions of the major legal scientists of the past, and 3)
the *Institutes*, a textbook for beginning students. Justinian's own

laws were added later in 4) a collection called his *Novels*. This whole restatement of Roman law was called the *Corpus Juris Civilis*.

The plan of reconquering Europe never succeeded, however, and the *Corpus Juris Civilis* was not promulgated in the west. The inhabitants of the former Roman Empire in the west simply had to get used to their German rulers. The Roman Law was not deliberately suppressed, though, for the Germans believed that law is personal, not territorial: a person keeps his or her native law regardless of who governs the territory. Germanic kings tried to give justice to their Roman subjects by means of Roman Law, and for this purpose they had abridgements made of the *Theodosian Code*. In areas where Germanic populations and culture least overwhelmed the Roman tradition, notably Italy and southern Gaul (Provence), Roman Law continued as a local customary law. Elsewhere in Europe, the Germanic customary laws of the invading peoples prevailed, except in regard to the Christian Church. She was a native Roman who could read, write, and remember, who was not mortal, and who valued the advantages conferred on her by the Roman Law, especially in the doctrines of corporation and sacred property.

Early in the 9th century one of the German kingdoms, that of the Franks, laid claim to the authority and even the name of the Roman Empire. Imaginatively and vigorously launched by Charlemagne in 800, the Holy Roman Empire by the 11th century had become strong and sophisticated enough to be a real rival to the Roman Christian Church in the field of international government. Both the Empire and the Church discovered the *Corpus Juris Civilis* of Justinian late in the 11th century, and both began quoting it and encouraging their supporters to study it, just as modern ideologists of the right and of the left claim and quote the same U.S. Constitution, hoping to make the ancient ideological authority their own.

A school of Roman Civil Law was endowed at Bologna in northern Italy about 1080. Here professors could study and organize the *Corpus Juris Civilis* and devise applications to modern condi-

tions; by this time the *Corpus* was half a millennium old. Here as
well students could learn sophisticated legal theory and prepare
themselves for excellent careers in the imperial civil service or
the church hierarchy. The first lecturer at Bologna was a German
named Werner, or in Latin, Irnerius. He was followed by a number
of hard-working commentators who blazed a trail of explanations
and cross-references through the jungle of the *Corpus Juris Civilis*.
In the middle of the 12th century a professor named Accursius
edited a complete marginal commentary called the Ordinary Gloss.

   The law courts of the German Empire and also of the northern
Italian city states and southern France (areas where Roman Law
had never completely died out) recognized, adopted and enforced
the newly revived Civil Law. Other universities hired professors
from Bologna to lead their own graduate faculties and began to
offer the degree LL.D., the Doctorate of Laws. Even in countries where Civil Law was not the law of the land, this sophisticated
legal science constituted the only academic course in theoretical
jurisprudence. Some Civilians (as the experts in Roman Law were
called), especially the famous Bartolo da Sassoferrato in the 14th
century, made a career of explaining the Civil Law answers to
legal problems such as alluvial rights and the conflict of laws,
thereby encouraging a broader acceptance of Civil Law principles.

   In the Age of the Renaissance – roughly the 15th century and
the early 16th – ancient Roman civilization was admired again
for its own sake, and European cultures tried in many ways to
imitate it. Roman Law became respectable in lands where it had
never been in force. The Civil Law remained the dominant
background for European legal history, and it strongly influenced
all the legal reforms in the revolutionary and nationalistic
reconstructions of Europe from the French Revolution of 1789
through the 19th century.

B. Civil Influences on British Law

   Roman Civil Law was never the law of the land in England.
English kings and judges usually considered it a foreign influence;

they were suspicious of it, and correspondingly proud of the
Common Law, England's home-grown answer to the *Corpus Juris
Civilis*. Nevertheless, the Civil Law has constantly influenced
English law in many official and casual ways.

One permanent Roman Law influence came through the clergy,
the professional personnel of the church. The church's legal traditions included Civil Law, and the Latin language of the *Corpus
Juris Civilis* made it accessible to them; Latin was the badge of
the clergy everywhere in the Middle Ages, even in England. With
a few important exceptions, nothing was written in medieval
Europe but in Latin, and nobody could read but the Christian
clergy. Consequently, any legal writing and record-keeping had
to be done by the "clerks", and they unintentionally did a lot of
translating of Common Law into Civil and Canon Law terms and
ideas. Some historians even claim that the earliest writs of the
Common Law were based on Civil Law processes.

Other influences are even clearer. The Lord Admiral of England
had a court from the middle of the 14th century, which judged
commercial and marine cases. Because the foreign traders had
grown familiar with Civil Law, and had adopted much of the law
of the *Digest* into their trading custom, called the Law Merchant,
Civilians were admitted as advocates in Admiralty. Until the 19th
century, such matters as contracts of marine insurance and temporary corporations simply could not be judged in England except with the help of the Civil Law. Besides the Court of Admiralty,
the Law Merchant had other courts and areas of influence toward
Civil Law. Any seaport or annual fair, and of course London, the
financial center of the country, had to be able to enforce merchants'
contracts and notes, and this meant having courts like the Piepowder
Courts (for the dusty-footed traders), which were familiar with
continental law, i.e. Civil Law.

The English courts that did not operate by Common Law had
to judge by "equity" or commonsense fairness; a judge in equity,
looking around for inspiration, as often as not found it in the Civil
Law, and many English practitioners were well trained in that
foreign commodity. In the 12th century the popes had tried to

prevent the teaching of Civil Law at Oxford University (like all the earliest Universities, Oxford had a papal charter), and Henry I forbade schools of Civil Law in London. Both prohibitions were practically ignored. Both Oxford and Cambridge Universities had graduate law faculties, and for six centuries these were exclusively Civil and Canon Law faculties, while English Common Law was not taught in any University. Henry VIII endowed chairs of Civil Law — the Regius (Royal) Professorships — at both Universities, and on the high tide of the Renaissance it seemed that the royal law of the future in England might well be Civil Law. The Common Lawyers fought back successfully, but Civil Law was entrenched until 1875 in Doctors' Commons, a college of LL.D.'s housed in St Paul's Churchyard, London, with exclusive competence in a few old Canon and Civil Law matters, especially Admiralty, Probate, and Divorce.

The other kingdom on the island, Scotland, had its own customary law, and in the 16th century the Scottish courts adopted a Civil Law restatement of it. The crowns of England and Scotland were united in 1603, when James VI of Scotland became James I of England as well, and at the beginning of the 18th century the parliaments were united as well. Even then, Scots Law remained independent, and Scottish lawyers working in England were a constant source of Civilian ideas.

The influences and the language that English law had borrowed from Civil Law were exported to North America in Blackstone's *Commentaries* (1763) on the eve of the American Revolution. A few scholars of the Civil Law, most notably New York's Chancellor Kent (d. 1847) influenced American jurisprudence somewhat in Civilian directions, but for North Americans today the major fields of activity for the Roman Law tradition remain Quebec, Louisiana and International Law.

Suggested Reading

A good discussion of the substantive influence of Civil Law is the one by the late Oxford Regius Professor H. F. Jolowicz, *Roman*

Foundations of Modern Law (Oxford, 1957). A brisk survey is provided by John Henry Merryman, *The Civil Law Tradition: An Introduction to the Legal Systems of Western Europe and Latin America* (Stanford, 1969). Paul Vinogradoff, *Roman Law in Medieval Europe* (2d ed. Oxford, 1929, repr. London, 1968) is a classic account by regions; for England, see pp. 97-119. The rather surprising Scots Law story is in Thomas B. Smith, *Scotland: the Development of its Laws and Constitution* (London, 1962), especially pp. 1-24 of the "Historical Background".

Terminology

actor [L] in Civil Law, the one who brings a lawsuit or action, the "plaintiff"; the plural is *actores*. Cf. *reus*.

censor [L] an officer of the Roman republic who kept the tax list or *census* and the list of the Senators. The *censor* could remove a name from a list at his pleasure, especially for reasons of public turpitude. Hence our usage *to censor* and *censure*.

client [LE] in ancient Roman society, a person socially and politically dependent on a patron; the patron would appear for his clients in litigation.

code [LE] from *codex,* a book bound in the modern way rather than a *volumen* or scroll. The title of official compilations of law by the emperors Theodosius (438 AD) and Justinian (534 AD).

curia [L] from *coviria,* "assembly of men", the name of the Senate hall in Rome, later applied to any sovereign assembly; not really the Latin original of **court,** q.v. above in chapter 3) but often used as if it were.

edict [LE] "declaration", by a Roman *praetor* or elected judge, of the new remedies he would provide in his court; later a permanent compilation of those equitable reliefs.

federal [LE] relating to the union of Rome with its allies in Italy by *foedera,* or treaties.

forensic [LE] "of the forum", q.v.; "judicial".

forum [L] the central marketplace of Rome, site of its daily civic business and its earliest lawcourts.

litigation [LE] from *lis* (plural *lites*), a formal judicial process, brought by the *actor* and contested by the *reus*.

magistrate [LE] the Latin *magistratus* meant "the superiority" [of the public over private interests], temporarily held by elected officials in Rome. The word also meant an officer who wielded this superior authority. These positions were primarily executive, only secondarily judicial.

plebiscite [LE] from *plebis scitum,* "opinion of the common people", a popular referendum proposed by the tribune, which could make laws even against the will of the Senate.

public [LE] from *poplicus* or *publicus,* "of the whole people (*populus*)" of Rome, not of any one person, however powerful.

republic [LE] from *res publica,* "the public business".

reus [L] the one charged with a crime or private wrong, "defendant"; also, "guilty", and so *mens rea,* q.v. in chapter 12.

riparian rights [LE] a category of Roman land law dealing with properties along a river bank, *ripa*.

senate [LE] the Latin *senex* means "old man", and *senatus* the public function of old men: the Roman council of state made up of the most senior citizens.

stipulation [LE] the old Roman form of oral contract, made in public by the two parties, each of whom would accept *verbatim* the terms spoken by the other: "Will you give this for such a price?" "I will give it. Do you promise to pay such a price?" "I promise." Later the term for a specific point of agreement by the parties to a contract or the attorneys in a lawsuit.

tribunal [LE] the bench or court of a Tribune (*tribunus*), the protector of the rights of the common people in the city districts (*tribus* or tribes).

usufruct [LE] the Civil Law category for one level of right in property, the "use of its fruits" without right to alienate it.

Chapter Five

Contracts and Debts

The Roman Empire developed an effective and sophisticated law of contracts, the kind that it needed as the center of an international market economy. Late medieval Europe, once it had recovered that advanced sort of economy, eagerly adopted the Roman Civil Law and incorporated much of it into the international Law Merchant. By contrast, England had a land-based economy when its Common Law was first developing, and the Common Law did not bother at all with contracts. As contractual problems developed in England, the Common Law responded by trying to treat contractual obligations as if they were interests in land, and breaches of contract as if they were trespasses, a very clumsy adaptation. Early in the 17th century England began to develop a new law of contracts which did not depend on the old fictions. Instead it drew on the Law Merchant and the Civil Law for its ideas and for a good deal of its terminology. That is why the wordlist for this chapter has so much language derived or borrowed from the Latin of the Civil Law, and so little Law French from the courts of Common Law.

For the references to maxims from the *Digest* and *Liber Sextus* which appear first in the following list, see chapter 17.

Terminology

ab initio [L] "from the beginning"; a contract can be void *ab initio* or can become void *ex post facto* (see chapter 23 and the maxim

Quod ab initio ... in chapter 20).

accede [LE] from the Latin *ad* + *cedere:* "yield to", "consent".

acceptance [LE] from the Latin *ad* + *cipere:* "a taking", and thereby implying agreement to the conditions attached to the giving.

accommodation [LE] an action "to the benefit (*commodum*)" of another, not for a consideration.

accord [LE] a contract for solution of an injury, bringing "heart to heart (*ad cor*)".

acquiescence [LE] "becoming quiet toward" a transaction, giving it tacit and passive approval.

aleatory [LE] "with dice (*alea*)" or "gambling", said of a contract in which performance is contingent on an uncertain event. A lottery ticket represents an aleatory contract, and so does a casualty insurance policy.

Aliud est celare, aliud tacere. [L] "To conceal is one thing, to be silent another." Broom (p. 781) explains succinctly that in a contract of sale "either party may ... be innocently silent as to grounds [for finding fault] open to both to exercise their judgement upon." If the bread for sale is visibly green, the baker is not bound to warn that it is old.

amortization "bringing toward death (*ad mortem*)", the gradual reduction of the agreed value of an asset over its useful life, until it finally has no value at all.

arrears [LFE] debts "behind (*arrière*)" in payment.

assign [LE] as a verb, "point to (*ad* + *signare*)": to transfer; as a noun, an assignee.

assumpsit [L] "he undertook", an early English writ to enforce contracts that were not under seal, were oral, or were merely implied, like the one between a barber and his customer. *Indebitatus assumpsit* was a writ of debt: "Being indebted, he undertook".

attachment [GFE] from the Old French *estachier,* "a nailing down", a seizure by court order. Stake is cognate to this word.

avoid [LFE] from the Latin *ex* + *vacuum* through the Old French *esvuidier* "to make empty": to make a contract, a judgement, or some other legal act **null and void** ("nothing and empty"). The word's similar sound and usage caused it to slip into the meaning of evade in vernacular English.

badges of fraud [L>E] recognized suspicious signs, such as fictitious consideration, or aliases for the parties, which justify a presumption of fraud. This strange phrase was suggested by the maxim *Dolum ex indiciis perspicuis probari convenit:* "Fraud ought to be proven by clear badges".

bankrupt [GIFE] "broken bench", "broken bank", a term for "insolvent" in the international Law Merchant. An early banker was a trader and contractor with a fixed stall or bench in some trading exchange. If he defaulted, his place of business would be literally or figuratively broken up (*ruptum*) by his colleagues.

bona fides; bona fide [L] "good faith"; "in good faith". The first is used as a noun, the other as an adjective or adverb.

breach of contract [GE;LE] note that this figure of speech takes a contract to be a bond between the parties which one of them can break by non-performance.

chose in action [F] "a thing in action", an intangible property, i.e. a right, which can be brought to court, while a *chose in possession* is a real thing in hand. (Alderman, pp. 1113-1114).

consensus ad idem [L] "consent to the same thing", a meeting of minds in making a contract.

consideration [LE] originally a word for star-gazing (Latin *sidera* = "stars"), consideration can mean contemplation or the thing contemplated. In English contract law from the 17th century, it is the prospective gain that a contractor has an eye on, the *quid pro quo* (q.v.) necessary for a contract and for its legal enforcement.

contract [LE] the "drawing together (*cum* + *tractus*)" of parties to business, a legal bond between them, obliging both.

creditor [LE] "believer", a lender, who believes in the debtor, trusting him to pay back a loan.

damages [LFE] the value or quantity of a loss, in Latin *damnum*. And see **compensatory damages** in chapter 6.

debt, debtor [LFE] what is owed (*debitum*), the one owing it.

default [LFE] failure (Latin *de* + *fallere*) to pay a due.

delivery [LFE] from the Latin *de* + *liber*; "freeing", "release" of goods to their rightful owner; once also the release of a prisoner from jail.

discharge [LFE] "unload", to unburden from debt or bankruptcy. The Latin *carrus* meant "cart"; the Late Latin *carricare* meant "to carry freight".

distrain [LFE] from the Latin *dis* + *stringere,* to take and hold as a pledge for performance. The act is called a **distress**.

ex contractu [L] "from a contract", one source of causes of actions; the other is *ex delicto* (see chapter 21).

Ex dolo malo non oritur actio. [L] "From a bad fraud no action arises". A party who gained a contract by deception cannot enforce it in court. See *dolus malus* in chapter 17.

Ex nudo pacto non oritur actio. "From a bare agreement no action arises." Broom (p. 745): Where there is no **consideration** (q.v. above) there is no real contract.

exoneration [LE] from the Latin *ex* + *onera*) "unburdening" from an expense, duty, or the weight of an accusation.

Ex turpi causa non oritur actio. "From a dirty cause no action arises". Broom (p. 731) summarizes that "an agreement to do an unlawful act cannot be supported at law".

garnishment [GFE] "putting under guard (Middle French *garnir*)": a judgement which attaches goods held by a third party to satisfy a debt.

gift [GE] a gratuitous assignment, without consideration.

hold harmless [L>E] under a contract, to promise indemnity to the other party: "The seller holds the buyer harmless"; often used as an adjective for a clause or agreement that does so: "the contract includes a hold-harmless clause". The phrase translates the Latin *tenere incolumem.*

illusory promise [LE] one that plays a trick (Latin *lusus*) by committing the promisor to nothing.

inchoate [LE] "just begun (*inchoatum*)", not fully formed, unfinished. The contrary adjective might be **executed** (of a contract), **registered** (of an instrument), or **mature** (of any right). Some ignorant persons have used *choate* as if it were a word, meaning the opposite of this one.

indemnity [LE] from the Latin *in* + *damnum*: "freedom from loss".

insolvent [LE] unable to break (Latin *solvere*) the bonds of debt.

joint and several [LFE] characterizes a liability for debt as belonging to a whole group (Latin *junctim,* joined together) and to each member of it (Latin *separatim*).

jurat [L] "he swears", used as a noun for the clause of an instrument in which a notary or court officer certifies the authenticity of its signatures and seals.

liable [LFE] from the Latin *ligabilis*, "able to be bound", owing a debt.

loan [NE] originally a gift or grant (Old Norse *lan*), later only a temporary one.

mala fides; mala fide [L] "bad faith"; "in bad faith".

meeting of minds [GE] a modern phrase describing one condition for a valid contract: *consensus ad idem* (q.v.).

Modus et conventio vincunt legem. "Custom and contract overcome law." Stated as a rule of law (no. 85) in the *Liber Sextus* of Boniface VIII; Broom (pp. 690-698) exhausts the subject and quotes Erle, J. in summary: "Parties to contracts are to be allowed to regulate their rights and liabilities themselves."

non est factum [L] "it was not done", the defense that an instrument of contract was not actually made; especially if a party signed it mistaking it for something else.

novation [LE] "making a new [contract]" by substitution of a new person for one of the parties.

nudum pactum [L] "bare agreement", less than a contract, lacking consideration, q.v. above. The plural would be *nuda pacta*. Cf. the maxim above, *Ex nudo pacto* ...

nulla bona [L] a return by a sheriff to a writ of execution, reporting that there are "no goods" to satisfy the judgement.

operative words [LE,GE] within a contract or other instrument, the precise words by which the purpose of the document is accomplished. The Latin *operare* means "to work".

pari passu [L] "on an even footing", said of creditors who are equal, not ranked in priority for payment.

party [LFE] The Latin *pars* means "fraction", one side of a relation, contract, political rivalry, or lawsuit.

peppercorn [HLE/GE] a grain of black pepper, representing minimal or merely nominal definite value, as in "a contract with only a peppercorn of consideration".

persona [L] in ancient drama, a stage mask that the actor "sounded through"; then a role in a play; a human being with particular interests and an independent place in society; now, a person is any entity recognized by law as existing and having rights. Neither is the singular of *people*.

privity [LFE] a person's having or sharing a dignity or property right; also, a piece of personal secret knowledge. The Latin privum means "peculiar", "individual".

quantum valebant [L] "as much as [certain goods] were worth", the statement of award in an implied contract of sale. Cf.*quantum meruit* in chapter 17.

quid pro quo [L] "something for something", the consideration in a contract.

Qui facit per alium facit per se. "He who acts through another acts himself." Principals are liable for the acts, including contracts, of their agents. The rule from the *Liber Sextus* (no. 72) is considered at length by Broom, pp. 816-842.

Qui sentit commodum sentire debet et onus. "The one who enjoys the advantage should also bear the burden." *Liber Sextus* rule 55, which Broom (pp. 705-712) applies especially to the responsibility of a tenant for general maintenance of a property.

rescind [LE] "to cut back (*re* + *scindere*)", to annul a contract as being void *ab initio* (q.v.). The act of doing so is **rescission**, and the incorrect form **recision** is sometimes seen.

salary [LE] "for salt (*sal*)", the cash pay of a Roman soldier to supplement his wheat and wine ration. So, a periodical cash compensation to an employee.

sale [NE] from the Old Norse *sala*: the action and ritual of exchange.

status quo [L] "the condition in which" a thing or person stands or stood: a quick way of referring to a complex condition of a particular moment that is to be maintained or restored. The adverbial phrase *in statu quo* is also used, and either phrase can be specified with … ante, "… before".

subrogation [LE] "a calling instead (*sub* + *rogatio*)", the substitution of one person for another in a right or claim. Note the doublet **surrogate** in chapter 8.

sui juris [L] "of his/her/their own right", not for another, not under another's guardianship. The contrary phrase is *alieni juris*, "of another's right".

surety [LFE] from the Latin *securitas* through the French *sureté*: the condition of being sure, and a person who is bound for another's debt in case the latter fails to pay.

time is of the essence: this phrase means not only that speed is important, but that failure to meet a specified deadline is a breach of contract. The phrase *de essentia,* "of the essence", occurs frequently in medieval philosophy in contrast to "circumstantial" and "accidental".

uberrima fides [L] "the fullest good faith"; the adjective phrase *uberrimae fidei,* "of the utmost good faith", describes a contract, e.g. of life insurance, which is **vitiated** (q.v. below) by any concealment or misrepresentation on the part of the purchaser.

usury [LE] "for use", once any premium paid in return for a loan of money, and frowned on by Biblical (Leviticus 25:37) and Canon

Law. Medieval Christians could not lend money to other Christians at interest, and so Jews were allowed to engage in that much-needed business. **Usury** is still the name for a wrongful act, but it now means only excessive **interest**, q.v. in chapter 18.

vitiated [LE] deprived of validity by some fault (*vitium*) or flaw. A contract may be said to be vitiated by fraud, or a marriage vitiated by an already existing marriage.

void [LFE] from the Latin *vacuum* through the French *voide:* "empty", entirely without legal validity, as a contract or a marriage may be. A **voidable** action is valid, but has a fault in it on account of which it can be nullified by judgement.

Chapter Six

Judgement and Enforcement

The terms in the following wordlist have some connection with the later stages of formal judicial process, after the pleadings are complete: verdict and judgement, execution orders and appeal. The maxim **Res judicata** ... below, and certain terms in later chapters (**estoppel** in 17, **agent** in 18, and **negligence** in 21), were used as instances of decaying legal communication by Wilfred K. Fullagar, "Legal Terminology", *Melbourne University Law Review* 1 (1957) 1-8.

Terminology

additur [L] "it is added", the power of a court to increase a jury's award; and the power of an appeals court to set a higher award which the defendant may accept and so avoid retrial.

adjective law [LE,NE] the law of procedure, "lying alongside (Latin *ad + jacitum*)" the substantive law.

adjudication [LE] the formal giving of judgement, the determination of a suit.

appeal [LFE] from the Latin *ad + pellare:* "to call [someone to answer a charge]", in feudal law, a challenge to judicial battle, now a process of retrial. The **appellant** makes an appeal against an **appellee** or **respondent** in a court of **appellate** jurisdiction. See Charles Rembar's essay on appeal and battle and their late survival in *The Law of the Land* (New York, 1980), pp. 18-35.

auditor [LE] "hearer", the president of some church courts; also a judge delegated to hear the accounts of tax collectors and stewards; hence an official supervisor of accounts.

bailiff [LFLE]. The old Latin *bajulare* meant "to carry"; the French *baillier*, "deliver [in trust]", and the **bailiff** (in Latin *baillivus*) was the court's receiver of bailments for appearance and payment of fines.

below [NE] "in the inferior court", a short way for an appellate court to speak of activities in a lower court from which a case has been appealed.

brutum fulmen [L] "dry thunder", a void judgement that might sound terrific, but does nothing judicially. The plural would be *bruta fulmina*.

citation [LE] "the act of rousing", summoning (Millar, p. 1025); and the act of calling attention to a published text such as a law report in support of a statement.

cognizance [LFE] official "recognition", jurisdiction over particular matters, or a judge's recognition, in a lawsuit, of facts not offered in evidence, also called judicial notice.

comity [LFE] from the Latin *comes*, "a comrade"; "friendliness", "agreeableness": the willingness of one sovereignty to accommodate the interests of another in its own territory; or (judicial comity) of a court to respect the decisions of other courts.

compensatory damages [LE,LFE] damages "weighing the same (Latin *com* + *pensum*)", i.e. limited to the loss. A **punitive** or **exemplary** award may be added to the compensatory damages, with the intention to punish or to make an example of the un-successful defendant.

contumacy [LE] "stubbornness", failure to appear when sum-moned, or obey when ordered, by a court. The Latin *tumeo* means "to swell up" like a bullfrog; *contumax* is "stubborn".

declaratory [LE] "making clear"; a declaratory judgement or relief establishes the rights of the plaintiff while making an award to satisfy them.

derogation [LE] from the Latin *de + rogare,* "call back": the par-tial anullment of a law by a later law, or of a precedent by a later judgement.

dictum [L] "something said"; the plural is *dicta.* Used as short for *obiter dictum,* "something said by the way", this refers to the portion of the text of a judgement which is not essential to the decision, and is not binding.

en banc [GF] the judges of a court sitting or deciding "as a bench", not singly; and as a full bench, not only a quorum.

enforcement [LFE] the application of coercion in support of a law or judgement. The Latin *fortis* means "strong".

error [LE] "a wandering" judgement or belief; ground for judicial review and reversal.

execution [LE] from the Latin *ex + secutum:* "following through" on a contract, court decision, or will, or on the laws, as the executive branch of government does.

fieri facias or *fi. fa.* [L] "you should cause [the amount of an award] to be made" by sale of goods belonging to the unsuccessful defen-dant; this is a writ of execution to a sheriff.

hard cases [GE,LE] cases in which commonsense fairness goes against legal principles. "Hard cases make bad law" by making anomalous precedents.

infant [LE] From the Latin *in* + *fans:* "not speaking": a baby too young to talk, or a minor without full legal personality (see ***persona*** above in chapter 5) and without the capacity to speak in court. The class also once included most women.

in pais [F] "in the country", known to the neighborhood and so to a jury, but not in the record or in writing, e.g. an **estoppel** (q.v. in chapter 17).

in personam [L] "upon the person", an action or judgement directed at a person and personal rights. Note that the similar *in persona* means "in person", e.g. an appearance in person, not with an attorney as substitute.

in rem [L] "upon the thing", an action or judgement directed at a property.

Interest reipublicae ut sit finis litium. [L] Well translated by Broom (p. 330): "It is for the public good that there be an end to litigation". Broom explains that a second trial should only be granted if the verdict of the first was faulty by the law or the evidence, not because of ineptitude on the losing side. He includes the doctrine of **estoppel** under this maxim (see chapter 17).

leading case [GE,LE] one that is recognized by judges as having definitively settled a particular legal question.

lie [GE] "exist", "be there", as in the sentence "If you fall down my stairs, an action for damages lies against me."

limitation [LE] the setting of a boundary (Latin *limes*): of time for actions to be brought under a **statute of limitations,** or of the degree of an **estate** (q.v. in chapter 15).

mandamus [L] "we command", one of the **prerogative** writs (ch. 23), ordering a public officer to do his duty on behalf of the petitioner.

master [LFE] The Latin *magister,* French *maître:* "teacher", "expert" to whom a court refers particular questions and tasks; or the employer of a servant.

nominal [LE] "named", "in name (Latin *nomen*) only", titular or minimal. Nominal damages might be awarded when a defamation is found by the jury, but the plaintiff had no reputation to lose.

non obstante veredicto, n.o.v. [L] "the verdict notwithstanding", a judge's award contrary to the jury's verdict.

nunc pro tunc [L] "now as if then": an act may be performed or registered retroactively so as to have the same effect as if it had been done or recorded earlier.

partial [LE] "in part" or (e.g. of a judge) leaning toward one party.

peers [LFE] The Latin *pares,* French *pairs:* "equals", especially members of a court selected to judge their equals, as provided in Magna Carta.

per curiam [L] "by the court" unanimously, without dissent.

pro forma [L] "for the sake of form", not of substance.

pro hac vice [L] "for this occasion", a permission for one time only.

pursuant to [LFE] The Latin *persequens*, French *poursuivant:* "following" or "in the course of doing".

ratio decidendi [L] "reason of the decision", the language of a judgement that declares its grounds. The plural would be *rationes decidendi*.

ratio legis [L] "the reason of the law", as sometimes expressed in a preamble to legislation, or as determined by research into legislative intent. "Reasons …" would be *rationes*; "… of the laws", *legum*.

remittitur [L] "it is sent back": the reduction of a jury's award for damages; or a **remittitur of record**, the sending back by an appeals court of the record of a case to the court below for a new trial or for execution of an appellate decision.

Res judicata pro veritate accipitur. [L] "Once a thing has been adjudged, it is taken as true", *Digest* rule 207, the ground of an exception in Civil Law and a modern absolute bar of action (see Fullagar, p. 7).

sequester [LE] to place a property in trust (Latin *secus* = safe) pending litigation.

sound in [LFE] in such legal expressions as "Detinue sounds in recovery, but libel sounds in damages", the phrase means "to echo", "to have legal consequences".

Stare decisis et non quieta movere. [L] "To abide by things decided and not to disturb peaceful things." This is a notion foreign to the Civil Law, essential to Common Law.

sub judice [L] "under the judge": *lite pendente* (q.v. above in chapter 3) and not yet determined.

supersedeas [L] "you should supersede", a writ to stay an execution or judgement, usually pending appeal.

viva voce [L] "with the living voice", orally.

Chapter Seven

History II: Canon Law and Jus Commune

The legal tradition of the Christian Church, from its beginning, was deeply Jewish. Both traditions consider obedience to law a religious virtue, and the will of God the ultimate sanction of the law. Ritual and dietary regulations; marital rules; equity and protection for the powerless; the status and behavior of religious leaders; crime as sin, a stain or deformation of the spiritual character; the protection of religious communities: these and other points of similarity show the debt of Christianity to the Jewish tradition of law.

A persecuted minority for three centuries, Christianity became fully legal under Roman Law in 313 AD, then rapidly rose to the position of the established religion of the Empire, stepping into the status of the former polytheistic state religion. The Church's privileges were codified in the Civil Law by Theodosius in 434 AD, and the Christian Church in the Middle Ages was the only religion with legal rights in Europe. Christian law, called Canon Law after the Greek word for "rule" or "standard" was at first confined to religious, ritual and moral topics, and was locally legislated and regulated, but when the Roman Empire collapsed in the 4th century, more and more responsibility for general social order fell on Church institutions, and they had more need for legal self-

defense. When German kingdoms succeeded the Roman governing institutions of western Europe, the very existence of the Church
(a permanent corporation under Roman Law) was threatened by
Germanic legal traditions that had no notion what a corporation
might be. For the sake of solidarity, the various local churches
began gravitating to the authority of the court of the Bishop of
Rome, the Pope, who could give law and justice to all.

When the *Corpus Juris Civilis* reappeared in Europe in the 11th
century, the German Emperors and the Popes both tried to
domesticate it, but the Emperors naturally had more success; this
was imperial law, after all. The Church had to organize its own
law in the same ways, that is, with definitive textbooks, University faculties, and hundreds of local courts all using the same law
code, to prevent its being merged into the secular international
authority. The first part of the Church's answer was provided by
a monk named Gratian, who had been trained in Civil Law at
Bologna. About 1140, Gratian published his *Decretum,* a full collection of traditional Canon Law texts arranged in an easy-to-use
topical order like that of Justinian's *Codex.* Using the *Decretum*
as a textbook, European universities developed faculties of Canon
Law and offered the degrees D.D. (Doctor of Decrees), J.C.D.
(Juris Canonici Doctor) and, for the really ambitious, J.U.D. (Juris
Utriusque Doctor, or Doctor of Both Laws, Civil and Canon).
New Canons continued to appear after Gratian, mostly decrees
in the form of letters by the Popes. The text of the *Decretum* was
brought up to date with official collections: the *Decretals* of
Gregory IX in 1234, the *Liber Sextus* of Boniface VIII in 1298,
and the *Clementine Constitutions* of Clement V in 1314.

Medieval Canon Law was not just a collection of helpful hints
for the pious, but a legal system with teeth. It had a monopoly
of some important fields of legal action, and its sanctions were
serious, even terrifying. The Christian clergy and religious persons were subject to it and to no other law. The Church courts
could not in principle shed blood, but they had prisons (penitentiaries) instead, as reformatories for the clergy. Canon Law claimed
jurisdiction over all sacred things, and the category of the sacred

included 1) church property (the largest class of real estate holdings in Europe); 2) *miserabiles personae* or wretched persons: widows and orphans, the poor, and weaponless serfs; 3) charitable trusts and the probate of wills; 4) all oaths, regardless of the occasion (contracts, elections, treaties, whatever). As well, of course Canon Law claimed jurisdiction over 5) sin; and until the 16th-century Reformation was the only law concerned with 6) marriage and legitimacy.

A person who was excommunicated from the Church by sentence of a court of Canon Law would do well to surrender and obey. Even if he could defy the threat of going to Hell, all his contracts and other legal relations ceased to exist with excommunication, and no Christian could stay under the same roof with him. Even kings and emperors caved in to that sanction.

Some canonical traditions became the property of other legal systems, especially after the Protestant Reformation of the 16th century. The pejorative term "casuistry", meaning special pleading, usually with religious overtones, comes from the school exercises in Canon Law and Civil Law in which the law was explained, not in the abstract, but in the context of *casus* — cases, events which might befall a party or might come before a judge in court. Hence our "cases", case law, and the case method of legal study. The strongest **subpoena** in the Middle Ages was "under pain" of excommunication from the Church, a truly fearsome penalty then, calculated to force attendance. The Inquisition has (and deserves) a bad name for its inhumanity to those suspect of heresy, but the same inquisitorial procedure, with the same Latin name, gives us the English **inquest**, a trial of evidence rather than a trial by ordeal. The common expression "without benefit of clergy" now describes an unblessed or casual marriage, but originally it characterized a death sentence that the convict could not evade by claiming "benefit of clergy", i.e. exemption from capital punishment as a Canon-Law privilege of those who could read and write.

The term *jus commune*, meaning "a common law", is sometimes used to designate the blending of Civil Law and Canon Law, especially in procedure, which began in the 14th century on the

Continent. The most important and widespread developments of *jus commune*, also called the Romano-Canonical tradition, came in the standardized forms of contracts and bonds, which could be enforced in either kind of court, and a private law procedure that had the best features of both systems.

When Henry VIII separated the Anglican Church organization from that of Rome in 1534, the Church Courts of England were nationalized and began a very long process of losing their jurisdictions, a trend that was not complete in England until the lay Court of Probate took over Wills in 1857. As the secular courts absorbed Canon Law business, they also adopted much substantial Canon Law, and its language remains a part of our legal terminology, attached to the topics that were the concerns of the medieval Christian Church.

The best treatment in English of the history of European *jus commune* is Engelmann's "Romano-Canonical Procedure", book III of his *History of Continental Civil Procedure* (1927), pp. 417-504.

Terminology

advocate [LE] "one called in (*ad + vocatus*)" as a patron in a lawsuit in ancient Rome, or as a champion for a non-fighting person, such as a church, in a medieval trial by battle.

approach the bench [L>E] translates *se appropinquare ad bancum,* an informality which was permitted in the summary civil processes of the *jus commune*.

beneficial interest [LE] the interest of the user of an estate, not the holder of title. This is the kind of interest that a Christian pastor had in his church property, called his *benefice*: he could use its regular income for his support, but could not alienate the land.

calumny [LE] "slander". An *actor* in Civil Law, Canon Law, or *jus commune* had to take an oath *de calumnia,* swearing that this was not the reason for his action.

canon [HE] "rule", "standard"; an official list of regulations or norms.

clerk [HE] this form and its doublet **cleric** both come from the Greek *kleros* or "sharer", one supported on a public, then an ecclesiastical, fund or pension. Hence, a member of the official class of the church as contrasted with the **laity**, "the people". A literate professional, a record keeper.

devil's advocate [L>E] translates *advocatus diaboli*, a real officer of a court of Canon Law, who argues Satan's side of the question of whether a person deserves canonization to sainthood or not. His Infernal Majesty has no standing *in persona sua* in a court of Canon Law. The phrase also refers to a late medieval genre of handbooks of procedure in *jus commune*, which were set in the form of an lawsuit by Satan to recover possession of mankind. These moot manuals had titles like *Processus Sathanae* and *Processus Belial.*

doli capax [L] "capable of fraud", past the age (usually calculated as 7 years) of innocence.

peremptory [LE] literally "putting an end", final; hence, not allowing any delay, as a final summons or peremptory court order.

subpoena [LE] "under penalty", of which the worst in the Middle Ages was excommunication; a summons with a sanction (Millar, p. 1025).

unconscionable [LE] not permitted by conscience; this phrase, used in reference to contracts, reflects the moral inclination of Canon Law.

Chapter Eight

Wills and Estates

Throughout the Middle Ages, and well into modern times in England, the protection of the last will and testament has been a serious concern of church courts, and a subject much discussed by Canon Law. The reason is simple. A medieval Christian when dying would confess his sins and make the only sort of amends for them that he could, in his weak condition: a testament with charitable bequests to a church or churches, and with a priest as confessor, witness, and notary. Germanic customary law recognized no testament, but only the blood-descent of property in the male line, and so Canon Law had to protect the church's interest with the old Roman way of devising property after death.

The language surrounding the law of wills and inheritance is a mixture of French, the language of the heirs of the land in England, and Latin from the Roman Civil Law of testaments, which Canon Law kept alive in the church courts of probate.

Terminology

ab intestato [L] "[succession] from an intestate person", from one who had made no testament.

ademption [LE] "revocation" of a legacy.

administrator [LE] "one who serves", especially serves the estate of a deceased person. The feminine is **administratrix**. An administrator appointed in the testament is called its **executor/ executrix**.

affinity [LE] from the Latin *ad + fines*, "at the borders"; "a bordering on": a relation by marriage; cf. **consanguinity** below.

aliquot [L] "some amount", a fractional share of property in an inheritance.

animus testandi [L] "the intention to make a testament"; the adverbial phrase is *animo testandi*, "with the intention to make a testament".

assets [FE] the French *assez* means "enough", and so the resources of an estate considered enough to pay the legacies, or the resources of a corporation sufficient to cover indebtedness. According to the principles of estate administration and of double-entry bookkeeping, the resources are just enough, because assets equal liabilities.

assigns [LFE] variant of **assignees**, those to whom property is transferred, assigned, "marked (*ad + signatum*)".

autre vie [F] "another life", the term of some estates, as in the phrase *pur [pour] autre vie*.

bequeath [GE] from the Old English *be + cwethan*: "speak to", "declare": to pass on by an oral will, not a written one (which is why the phrase is not Latin); later, to pass movables by will. The noun is **bequest**.

causa mortis [L] "because of death", also found reversed, *mortis causa*; refers to acts done because of approaching death.

chattels [LFE] personal, movable property. The word was derived, like **capital**, from the Latin *capitale*, "of the head", "personal"; and the English word **cattle** is a further specialization.

collateral [LE] from *latera*, "sides": "alongside", with two legal meanings: 1) related horizontally (as sisters or first cousins), in contrast to **lineal**, e.g. mother and daughter; 2) property pledged for security of a loan or contract.

compos mentis [L] "in possession of his/her mind", mentally able to make a testament or contract; the obsolete *compos sui* was a broader category: "in control of himself/herself" or "free to act".

consanguinity [LE] "relation by blood (*sanguis*)", contrasted to affinity above.

contingent [LE] "touching", "depending", conditioned on an uncertain future event.

cum testamento annexo [L] "[administration] with a testament attached"; an appointment of an executor by the court of probate.

de bonis non [*administratis*]*, d.b.n.* [L] "[administration] of the goods not [yet administered]"; an appointment of a successive administrator.

decedent [LE] from the Latin *de + cedere*, "to withdraw"; "the one dying", a deceased person.

devastavit [L] "he wasted", a writ against a bad administrator, also used as a noun meaning the wasting itself.

devise [LFE] "divide", to give by will, now applied especially to real estate, while **bequeath** is reserved for movables.

distribution [LE] "a sharing out", the assignment of portions of an estate by the administrator; a receiver of a share is called a **distributee**.

eleemosynary [HLE] "as a charitable gift"; the old English cognate is **alms**.

endowment [LFE] the settling of a permanent gift on an institution, likened to a bride's **dower** (Latin *dos*), because the medieval endowments were to churches, whose bishops, like husbands, could use but not alienate the property.

heir [LFE] the Latin *heres* was the single successor to all the rights and liabilities of a deceased person, by relation or by appointment.

in articulo mortis [L] "at the point of death", when a giver is presumed to be disinterested; deathbed gifts and statements are characterized by this phrase.

in contemplation of death [L>E] translates the Latin *intuitu mortis* or *in contemplatione mortis*. Gifts so qualified do not evade estate taxes.

in esse [L] "in being", already born.

in posse [L] "in possibility", not yet in existence, unborn.

in terrorem [L] "intended to frighten", a clause in a will that threatens to disinherit anyone who contests the will.

in utero [L] "in the womb", an unborn life.

inter vivos [L] "among living persons", characterizing a gift completed before the death of the donor.

intestate [LE] "not having made a testament".

issue [LFE] from the Latin *exitus*, "that which has come forth": children; or the outcome of a course of pleading and answer in a lawsuit that brings the parties head to head, one affirming and the other denying the same thing. Then they have "joined issue". The Civil Law equivalent was the *litis contestatio*.

legacy [LFE] from the Latin *legatio*, "sending", bequeathing, a bequest. The receiver is a **legatee**.

Mobilia sequuntur personam. [L] "Movable goods follow the person." Broom, p. 522, applies this maxim by observing that it is the law of the place of the owner's domicile that covers the disposition and alienation of movables.

nuncupative [LE] "naming". A nuncupative will in Roman Civil Law was a soldier's will, brief and oral but binding, wherein he simply named his heir. Now, an oral will.

per capita [L] "by heads", a testamentary distribution of equal shares to all distributees, contrasted with *per stirpes* [L] "by branches", an equal distribution to each line of descent.

perpetuity [LE] "eternity", an estate controlled forever by a will, now prohibited.

probate [LE] from the Latin *probatio*, "proving", the process of establishing the authenticity and validity of a will, and then supervising its execution.

residuary [LE] "of the remainder (*residuum*)", referring to the legatee who is to receive all the property left after the fixed-sum bequests have been deducted.

reversion [LE] "a turning back", a future interest kept by a grantor of property.

settlor [GE] "establisher", the funder of an endowment.

sine prole [L] "without issue".

spendthrift trust [L+GE] a trust designed to keep the beneficiary from squandering an estate. The Old Norse *thrifask* meant "to thrive", to have plenty; the Latin *expendere*, "to squander".

surrogate [LE] "called instead (*sub* + *rogatus*)", "substitute". Because this was the name of a bishop's or chancellor's judge delegate, it is the title of the judge and court of probate in New York and some other states.

will [L>GE] from Old English *wille*, "wish", translating the Latin of the *Digest: ultima voluntas*, "last will".

Chapter Nine

Penal Law

In the Middle Ages, punitive sentences of imprisonment, whether indefinite, for life, or for a set term, were imposed only by church courts, as penances intended to reform the criminals. Church courts were not allowed to issue sentences that shed blood, killed or maimed, as the secular courts could, and so prisons (which we still call penitentiaries) were kept by bishops and abbeys to punish clerics and others convicted of ecclesiastical crimes. The English royal prisons and the sheriffs' county gaols kept prisoners only until they came to trial on a writ of *habeas corpus* or a circuit judge's commission of general gaol delivery, or for the short time between sentence and execution. The franchise prisons, kept by privileged nobles, served the same purposes, and they also held private prisoners of war awaiting ransom, prisoners who had not gone free on their **parole**. A debtor could be held in prison on a writ of *capias ad satisfaciendum*. The institution of guarded asylums goes back to lunatic asylums, leproseries, and the peculiar English custom of permanent sanctuary, for which see R.F. Hunnisett, *The Medieval Coroner* (1961).

Terminology

allocution [LE] "speaking to (*ad* + *locutio*)": the judge's question, addressed to the defendant after a guilty verdict, "Is there any reason why sentence of ... should not be pronounced on you?" The best and commonest answer, until it was abolished in England in 1827, was "I pray [the benefit of] my clergy", meaning "I can read and write in Latin, and so you can't hang, draw and quarter me."

arrest [LFE] "to halt (*ad* + *restare*)", also a noun. The essence of this act is the authoritative command, "Stop in the name of the law". **Arrest** also applied to things, and still does in Admiralty and Scots Law.

asylum [HLE] The Greek *asylon* means "inviolable place". A person in danger of death by revenge or law could be safe at almost any ancient Greek altar, because violence in a **sanctuary** was itself such a terrible crime. Similarly with Christian churches, whose protection the insane, orphans, and some felons could claim as a right.

atone [GE] "to make one again", restore a relation broken by an offense.

capital [LE] "of the head", especially a sentence of death.

captive [LE] "one taken (*captus*)", especially in war.

cell [LE] "little chamber", a monk's single room, and so a room in a penitentiary.

civil death the ceremonial divestiture of private property and rights that accompanied entry into a religious house by a monk, a nun, or a penitent. Also **attainder**, q.v. in chapter 16.

commutation [LE] "a complete change (*cum* + *mutatio*)", usually of a death sentence into something else.

correctional institution [LE] This phrase reflects the idea that imprisonment is for moral improvement, **rehabilitation**, as the monastic penitentiary was.

detention [LE] "holding away (*de* + *tentio*)", imprisonment for whatever reason.

determinate sentence one "fixed in length".

deterrent [L] "frightening (*de* + *terrens*)", also used as a noun, reflecting one theory of criminal punishment.

fine [LE] "end", the payment that closes a legal case; later, any payment to the state under legal compulsion.

gallows [GE] a German term, from Old High German *galgo*, for a Germanic method of judicial killing with deterrent humiliation.

incarceration [LE] "a putting in prison (*carcer*)", in the ancient Roman practice, either awaiting execution or for death by starvation.

jail [LGE] from the soldiers' Latin *caveola*, "little hole"; the British spelling has been **gaol** until recently.

outlaw [NE] from the Old Norse *utlagi*: one without the protection of his native law, whom anyone could kill or injure without retribution. Outlawry was part of the sentence in criminal judgements *in absentia*, a parallel to excommunication in Canon Law.

pardon [LFE] "forgive (*per* + *donare*)"; "forgiveness", a remission of punishment for crime.

parole [HLFE] "speech". As a Latin word, "informal chat", but in French a formal pronouncement; *parole d'honneur* was a promise by a person of honor, specifically a captured knight's promise that if set free he would not fight again until ransomed, and would return to captivity if called. Instead of **sequestering** a jury, the judge might put them on their parole not to discuss the case or read newspapers during a recess.

penitentiary [LE] from the Latin *paenitet*, "one regrets"; "a regretting place", "a place for penance": Canonical captivity.

prison [LFE] "taking (Latin *prehensio* to French *prision*)"; military captivity was **imprisonment**.

probation [LFE] from the Latin *probare*, "to test"; "proving oneself", another Canon Law notion.

recidivist [LFE] "one who falls back (*recidit*)" into sin or crime.

reformatory [LFE] "a place for reshaping" the character.

remorse [LFE] "a bite (*morsus*) behind", the pain of consciousness of one's past bad deeds.

reprieve [LFE] "taking a person back (French *repris*)" to prison instead of executing a death sentence.

retaliation [LE] the Latin *talio*, from *tale* ("like") meant "repayment in kind"; retaliation is the "eye for an eye" theory of criminal punishment, practically identical to [LE] **retribution** and [GFE] **revenge**.

stigma [HLE] "a brand", "mark of infamy", criminal reputation.

warden [GFE] "guard" is cognate.

Chapter Ten

History III: Germanic and French Custom, Feudal Law, and Law French

Most of the inhabitants of Europe when the Roman Empire fell in the 4th century AD belonged to the various Germanic nations. The Germans thought of law as part of their national heritage, almost part of their language, a heritage that a person was born into and carried for life, wherever he travelled. The Goths came from eastern Europe and settled with their Gothic law in Italy for a while, and even in Spain. Lombards kept their law when they moved into northern Italy. The Franks invaded Roman Gaul, and so completely dominated its Gaulish (Celtic) and Roman inhabitants that we call the territory now by the name of the Germanic invaders, France. The Franks, because they invaded in largely military, male, groups, took local wives when they settled down, and so their children grew up speaking the Romance language of the land (now named French) rather than the Germanic language of their fathers and their law. Fathers may lay down the law, but it is mothers who teach language.

The Germanic laws were never written down except by strangers. Charlemagne, for example, who needed law-texts to govern Germans other than his fellow Franks, ordered collections of their laws written down. Otherwise, the Germans kept their laws by customary observation and oral memory, preserved in poetic verses

and accompanied by their own ritual forms. The laws were kept
so tenaciously in memory by such means that we have dozens of
legal formulas imbedded in our Germanic language of English.
The pioneer folklorist Jacob Grimm initiated the joint study of
Germanic oral poetry and law with his essay "Von der Poesie im
Recht" in 1816. For example, "by hook and by crook" (meaning
"by any means possible") is an old way of referring to a limited
right to gather fuel in a lord's woodlot; the peasant could not cut
live wood with an axe, but could gather any twigs or dead wood
lying, hanging, or standing, that could be secured with a pruning
hook or a drover's crook. "To have and to hold" survives in the
formulas for acquiring possession of land or of a spouse, and so
does the French translation *a aver et tener*. Dramatic procedures
like the **moot** or "meeting", **wedding** with a **ring**, and the **oath**;
and customary rights like **thoroughfare**, often retain Germanic
names. *Burh*, meaning "defense" or "protection" gives us **borough,
burglary** (from burh-break), and also **borrow**, "to take on
security".

The customary law of the free, fighting Germans survived in
the Feudal Law, itself named after the *feof* or *fief*, land held by
the sword; hence both **fee** and **feud**. Feudal Law was the special
class law of the military caste of Europe from the 10th century
until the abolition of noble privileges in 1789, the crucial event
of the early French Revolution. The special interests of this military
caste were land inheritance, marriage alliances, and battle on
horseback for fun, for profit, and for justice. The members of the
caste were the **chivalry** or **cavalry**, the knights. England was invaded by French-speaking knights in 1066, and was governed by
that military upper caste, speaking the French language less and
less well, for several centuries. That is why there is such a thick
layer of French in the language of the law, and why a large number
of Law French words and phrases deal with those old concerns
of the Germanic customary law and the Feudal Law. To pick only
one example of this legacy, the Fifth Amendment to the US Constitution rejects **double jeopardy; jeopardy** recalls the **trial by
battle** or **wager of battle** that was the legal right of the knightly

class alone. They regarded it as an appeal to chance and to God, a *jeu parti*, "game with two sides".

The lawyers of England after the Conquest dealt mostly with the French-speaking aristocracy, and they practised their profession in French. But as time and political change separated the aristocracy further and further from their Norman and French past, they used English more and more for daily use, and their formal and legal French kept getting less and less like the language spoken in Paris. Strange as Law French became, it served the purpose of all jargon, protecting the exclusive professional franchise and information from outsiders. Pleading in French was sternly forbidden by the Statute of Pleadings in 1327, which required oral English and written Latin. The statute was ignored, and Law French continued to be used, sliding into sillier and stranger forms until Cromwell's Commonwealth passed a language reform act in 1650, which required both pleading and the record to be in English. This reform also failed. King George II tried again in 1731, and would likely have failed again, had it not been for the appearance in 1765 of Blackstone's *Commentaries*, the first authoritative English lawbook written in English. Law French has been considered antique ever since, and it is still in the process of disappearing.

Further Reading

References in this chapter and elsewhere have been made to the following articles: Sidney S. Alderman, "The French Language in English and American Law", *Canadian Bar Review* 28 (1950) 1104-1123. Theobald Mathew, "Law-French", *Law Quarterly Review* 54 (1938) 358-369.

Terminology

a aver et tener [GE>F] a Germanic law-jingle translated into Law French, and later into English, "to have and to hold".

attorney [FE] from the French *attourné,* "the one turned to", "the one appointed", a champion or representative.

champerty [LFE] from the French *champs parti,* "a shared field" of battle, a part in another's quarrel or lawsuit. This is the name for the lawyer's practice of taking contingent fees in those places, such as Ontario, where it is considered an offense; cf. maintenance below in chapter 11.

dehors [F] "outside", "foreign to", as in **dehors the record**. See Alderman, p. 1114.

feme covert or *feme sole* [LF]: *femme couverte,* misspelled in Law French, is "a woman covered [by her husband's rights]"; *femme sole,* "a woman alone".

fief, fee, feud [GFE] see the introduction to this chapter.

habendum [GE>L] the full phrase *habendum et tenendum* was record Latin for "to have and to hold"; therefore, the part of a deed which begins with that word and which defines the estate being granted.

jeopardy, double jeopardy [LFE] see the introduction to this chapter.

law [NE] from *lög,* one of the few Norse words in the English language, apparently not cognate to *lex* and **legal**.

mischief [LFE] from *mis* + *captio,* a wrongful causing of loss to another, trivialized in common English.

moot [GE] "assembly", and so a group trial or discussion, and the adjective meaning "debatable", and the verb meaning "argue" or "propose for discussion".

oath [GE] from *eid*, swearing with a sanction.

oyer and terminer [L>F] the Law French version of terms from an English judge's commission for criminal causes, *audire et terminare*, "to hear and bring to an end". So, circuit commissions and courts, often paired in England with **general gaol delivery**.

oyez [LF] Norman French from *audite*, "hear ye". Not related, as Blackstone supposed, to "oh yes".

purchase [LFE] from the Old French *purchacier*, "to chase after", any method of acquiring property other than inheritance.

rebuttal [GFE] "a beating back", physically, then orally in court.

service [LFE] the Latin *servire* meant "to be a slave"; the Old French *servir*, "to offer" as a servant offers a dish at table. Hence this courteous euphemism for the physical touching of a written summons to the body of the one summoned. By the etiquette of feudal society, any touch less indirect and polite could be taken as an insult and a cause of battle by a person of knightly rank.

thoroughfare [GE] from the Old English *thuruh faran*, "to travel through": public passage and a customary right of passage through private land.

Chapter Eleven

Domestic Relations

While the Christian Church radically changed the spirit of marriage in the Roman world in the process of converting it, the legal vocabulary with which Canon Law dealt with marriage and divorce, legitimacy and heritage, was the old Civil Law vocabulary. On account of the centuries of Canon Law monopoly in this area, we still have many of those terms in the secular law of domestic relations.

Terminology

a mensa et thoro [L] "from table and bed", "from bed and board". The Latin should properly be spelled *toro*, but it isn't. Divorce *a mensa et thoro* is a separation by law without judgement on the marriage.

a vinculo matrimonii [L] "from the bond of matrimony"; such a divorce dissolves the marriage contract. **Matrimony**, from the Latin *mater*, "mother", was the status of a woman which made her a Roman mother of Roman children.

abortion [LE] from the Latin *ab* + *ortus*, "mis-birth", a miscarriage, originally from whatever cause.

absolute [LE] "washed away (*ab* + *solutum*)", "complete", "without conditions"; specifically in relation to divorce, the final dissolution of the contract.

adoption [LE] "a selection (*ad* + *optio*)", "a choosing in": making a person one's legal child and heir by choice, not birth.

adultery [LE] originally, a wife's granting of marital advantages "to another (*ad ulterium*)" rather than to their owner, her husband.

alimony [LE] "for food", an allowance of the basic necessities to a separated spouse.

annulment [LE] "[reduction] to nothing (*ad nullum*)", a judicial decision that a legal condition does not exist at all.

ante-nuptial [LE] "before the veiling": legal marriage activities before the formal ceremony, especially contractual agreements. Latin had two phrases for "to marry": the man was said *ducere in matrimonium*, "to lead [his bride] into Roman motherhood"; the woman was said *se nubere*, "to veil herself".

bigamy [HLE] "having two marriages (Greek *bi* + *gamoi*)".

collusion [LE] "playing a trick together (*con* + *lusus*)", any agreement between adverse parties to take advantage of the court, e.g. by concocting evidence of adultery in a divorce which the defendant is only pretending to contest.

common law marriage It is actually a Canon Law marriage that is constituted by the consent of the parties and can be proven by public knowledge. This marriage by usage and reputation is also called a "Scotch marriage" because in Scotland the Canon Law of marriage was the customary law as well. There was no such thing as an English Common Law marriage.

community property [LE] the legal presumption that married partners both together own their total wealth; the usage of certain States. This usage can be supplanted by a contrary marriage contract.

condonation [LE] "a giving-in agreement (*con* + *donatio*)": one partner **condones** an offense of the other against the marriage by continuing or resuming the marital relation after finding out. Something like marital **laches**.

conjugal [LE] "related to the yoke (*jugum*) of marriage".

consortium [LE] "the sharing of one fortune (*sors*)".

consummation [LE] from the Latin *con* + *summare*, "to cap": the sexual union without which a marriage contract is not executed.

contumely [LE] "insulting behavior", less than actionable between strangers, but inofficious, i.e. contrary to duty, between spouses.

custody [LE] "guardianship".

divorce [LE] "turning apart (*dis* + *vertio*)", "a fork in the road".

dower, dowry [LFE] Both come from the Latin *dos*, and both meant the same originally: the bride's property, brought into marriage from her own family or given by her husband after marriage, which would remain hers upon divorce or his death. Now, **dowry** means the wealth brought by the bride into the marriage, and **dower** is what she can carry out of it, especially from a settlement by her husband.

emancipation [LE] "release from the hand". In Roman Law, almost all legal property, including wives, children, and slaves, was "in the hand" of fathers-of-families. What a *paterfamilias* had **mancipated**, "taken in hand", he could also formally and legally **emancipate**.

filiation proceeding [LE] a legal process to determine whose a child is: a paternity suit, from the Latin *filius* or *filia*, "son" or "daughter".

guardian [GFE] one legally responsible for the care of another. The one cared for is called by the cognate **ward**.

incest [LE] "uncleanness", an offense against a religious sense of decency, once a more general term, but now restricted to the sexual union of blood relatives.

in loco parentis [L] "in the place of a parent", with a parent's authority over a child.

maintenance [LFE] from the Latin *manum + tenere*, French *main + tener*, "hand-holding", any kind of support, especially of a dependent within a family. The term was also used for the treasonous **maintaining** of private armies of clients and supporters in England during the 15th-century Wars of the Roses. The patron of a "livery" would support them in court even in cases where he was not himself concerned, and this sort of interference with justice remained illegal long after the national emergency had passed. Cf. **champerty** above in chapter 10.

majority [LE] "state of being greater (*major*)", in number or in age; full legal age.

marriage settlement [LFE+GE] Although derived from the Latin *matrimonium* (as above under *a vinculo matrimonii*), **marriage**, like many other FE words ending in -*age*, refers to a quantity of payment, as in **average, carriage, portage, millage. Marriage** meant the agreement on the contract, including the dowry to be settled on the bride.

minor [LE] "less", especially "younger", not of legal age.

moiety [LFE] from the Latin *medietas*, "half", one spouse's share under **community property**, q.v. above.

next friend [GF>E] translates the Law French *prochein ami*, "nearest friend", a minor's representative in the absence of a guardian.

nisi [L] "unless". A *decree nisi*, as in a divorce action, is final unless, within a stated term, the defendant shows cause to over-turn it. Cf. *nisi prius* in chapter 14.

parens patriae [L] short for a maxim like this: The sovereign is "parent of the whole country", so that the state is responsible for the guardianship of the legally disabled. This was the medieval role of the church, protector of the *miserabiles personae*.

Pater is est quem nuptiae demonstrant. [L] "The father is the one whom the marriage points out", a presumption that a married woman's children are her husband's also. Broom, pp. 515-521, deals with the application of this maxim to legitimacy and heritage.

puisne [LF] "later born", referring to a son not the first, and sometimes to a judge not the senior one on a bench. Pronounced, and with other meanings spelled, *puny*.

putative [LE] "supposed (*putatum*)", especially under a presump-tion, as the maxim *Pater is est ...* above identifies a **putative** father.

recrimination [LE] "a blaming (Latin *criminatio*) back", a charge by an accused against the accuser, especially in a divorce action.

uxor, ux. [L] "wife".

Chapter Twelve

Crime

The linguistic cast of the following terminology shows the French-speaking, Latin-writing courts of medieval England reflecting on contemporary criminal disorder.

Terminology

abduction [LE] "leading away (*ab* + *ductum*)": either the kidnapping of a dependent or the seduction of a spouse.

abet [GFE] "to urge on" in a fight; **bet** means "to root for". This could be an offense, encouragement to a crime, as in the phrase **aid and abet**. One who does so is an **abettor**.

abscond [LE] "to hide away (*abs* + *condere*)", especially oneself, in one's house or by flight, often with movables of value.

accessory [LE] from the Latin *accessus*, "approach"; an adjunct, hence an assistant, particularly a person helping in the commission of a crime.

accomplice [LFE] "one folded in (Latin *ad* + *com* + *plicatus*)", involved in a crime.

actus reus [L] "a guilty act", half the requirement for criminal conviction (plural *actus rei*); the rest is **mens rea**, q.v.

alibi [L] "elsewhere", a claim that one was elsewhere at the time a crime was committed, used as a defense.

arson [LFE] from the Late Latin *arsio*, "burning".

blackmail [GE + NE] a payment in kind (not in silver, which would be **whitemail**); protection money and its extortion. Now usually narrowed to extortion by threat of criminal prosecution or mere publicity. The Old Norse *mal* meant "agreement".

bribery [FE] In Old French a *bribe* was a crust of bread, a hand-out to a beggar; then the corrupt receiving of goods, then the giving as well.

burglary [GELE] A German *burh* was a walled house or village; the Old English *burgh-brech* a breaking and entering, rendered in Latin as *burglaria*. The English legal term means especially a breaking in at night.

compounding [LFE] from the Latin verb *componere*, "to put together", "to agree"; settling for cash, especially the act of an official who takes money rather than prosecuting a felony.

connivance [LFE] "bringing the eyelids together (Latin *connivere*)", winking as a conspirator, or closing one's eyes to a crime that one should oppose.

conspiracy [LFE] "whispering (*spirare*) together".

constable [LFE] from the Latin *comes stabuli*, French *conestable*, "officer of the stable" in the French and English royal courts, and so the head of the household cavalry or police guard.

corpus delicti [L] "body of the crime", its physical, factual substance. "Bodies" = *corpora*; "of crimes" = *delictorum*.

counterfeit [LFE] "made in imitation (Latin *contra* + *factum*)", especially false coin.

crime [LFE] The classical Latin *crimen* meant any accusation; the Civil Law *crimen lesae majestatis* was a charge of treason, the "crime of wounding the greatness of the state". This general rationale stood behind the English notion of crime: offenses against the king's power and majesty, specifically murder of one of his subjects or robbery on the king's highway; cf. **lese majesty** in chapter 23.

crimen falsi [L] "a charge of lying": perjury or fraud. The plural would be *crimina falsi*.

culpable [LFE] from the Latin *culpa*, "guilt"; "blameworthy", guilty, especially with *mens rea*, q.v.

delinquent [LE] "leaving [a duty] behind"; neglecting appropriate action or behavior.

embezzlement [FE] from the Middle French *embeseiller*, "to destroy": "devastation" of an entrusted property.

embracery [FE] "setting on fire", attempting to influence a jury by threats or offers. The figure of speech seems to presume that a jury is as ready to sell its verdict as dry tinder is ready to catch fire if a "live coal" (*brase*) is touched to it.

extortion [LE] "wringing (*torsio*) out", the crime of compelling payments by violence or threat.

felony [LFE] The Latin *fel* means "gall", "bitterness"; the French *felon* means a venomous person, one whose mind is poisoned by his gall, a cruel ("fell") criminal; and felony is wickedness, now the worst degree of crime. *Felo de se* is a suicide or attempted suicide.

flagrante delicto [L] "while the crime was still blazing"; a culprit caught *in flagrante delicto* could also be said to be red-handed or to have a smoking gun.

forgery [LFE] The Latin *fabricare* meant "to manufacture", and

the French *forger* applies it especially to metalwork; the English
forgery is fabrication, false creation.

fraud [LE] from the Latin *fraus*, the wrong of deceit, especially
in a contract.

homicide [LE] "man-killing (*homo* + *cadere*)".

infraction [LE] "breaking" of a law or regulation.

investigate [LE] "to follow tracks (*vestigia*)".

kidnapping [NE] "seizing young goats", 17th-century slang for
snatching young people for transport as bound servants to the
American colonies.

larceny [LFE] The Latin *latro*, then the French *larcin*, meant
"thief".

locus poenitentiae [L] "a place to repent", opportunity to draw
back from a crime, or from a business agreement.

maim [FE] "to mutilate (Old French *maynier*)" the body; the noun
for the act is **mayhem**.

malum in se [L] "evil in itself" (plural *mala in se*), naturally
criminal.

malum prohibitum [L] "prohibited evil" (plural *mala prohibita*),
an act criminal by law though not by nature.

manslaughter [GE] "man-killing".

mens rea [L] "guilty mind": knowledge and intention to crime.
The plural would be *mentes reae*.

miscreant [LFE] "wrong believer (*mis* + *credens*)", originally
a condemned heretic.

misdemeanor [LFE] "misguiding oneself (Old French
misdemener)", misconduct; an offense less than a felony.

misfeasance [LFE] "wrong performance (Latin *facere*)" of a permitted action; cf. **malfeasance** in chapter 23.

misprision [LFE] from the Latin *mis* + *prendere*, Middle French *prision*, "wrong dealing", a vague offense, now usually limited to **misprision of felony**, the concealment of another's crime.

mitigating circumstances [LE] circumstances which make an offense "milder (*mitis*)".

murder [GE] from Old High German *mord*, unlawful killing.

particeps criminis [L] "one who takes a share of a crime". "Sharers" = *participes*; "of crimes" = *criminum*.

plagiarism [LE] The Latin *plaga* was a net, *plagium* the netting of game or the crime now called kidnapping, and *plagiarius* was a fowler; so **plagiarism** or **plagiary**, netting another's words and using them as one's own.

police [HLE] Greek *polis* means "city", and the Greek-Latin *politia* means "[public] policy", the management of a city, or its peace force.

Qui tacet consentire videtur. [L] "He who is silent seems to consent". This is *Liber Sextus* maxim 43. Broom (p. 138) interprets that tacit consent is **estoppel**, and (p. 787) that a contractor can commit fraud by tacitly allowing another's fraudulent representation to stand. Obviously a weak and convertible maxim.

rape [LFE] "snatching (Latin *raptio*)", "robbery", originally abduction, then sexual assault.

robbery [GE] from Old High German *roubön*, "to take by force"; wrongful taking of movables with violence or threat.

toxic [HLE] The Greek god Apollo was pictured causing epidemic diseases by shooting with a bow, *toxon*. The adjective **toxic** refers to killing from a distance by poison, and intoxication is poisoning, used especially for the effects of alcohol.

utter [GFE] an adjective equivalent to "outer", extreme; an English **utter barrister** was a junior counsel outside the bar, while King's Counsel could plead inside it. As a verb, "to put out", publish, offer to the public, e.g. the crime of **uttering** false money or negotiable instruments.

vagrancy [LFE] from the Latin *vagari*, "to wander"; the offense under the Elizabethan Poor Law of being a suspicious person, a sturdy vagabond with no visible means of support. A charge that can be used in combatting prostitution, unlicensed begging, mugging, etc. without the need to prove that such crimes were really committed or planned.

vandalism [GLE] The Vandals were a German tribe who migrated to the Mediterranean and sacked Rome in 455 AD. They were also Arian Christians — heretics in the eyes of the Orthodox Christians of Africa. Vandalism is the crime of behaving like the Vandals.

victim [L] from an Indo-European root meaning "holy", the Latin *victima* meant "a sacrificial animal", so the sufferer of violence or wrong. Victimization is a measure of crime by its harm to persons.

violation [LE] The Latin *vi* means "by force"; violence is the use of force, especially when unjustified; **violation** is a harm, especially to a law or regulation or to a person's rights or integrity, sometimes specifically by rape.

Chapter Thirteen

Documents, Instruments, and the Record

Germanic Customary Law had no tradition of written laws or written records, but the English in Britain and the Normans across the Channel, both under the influence of the Roman Church, had begun using written communications and records even before the Conquest of 1066. After the Conquest, writing proved so useful as a tool for the centralized legal control of the island that legal writing and the clerical profession quickly increased in importance and influence. England led northern Europe in the development of a Chancery whose writs were available throughout the country to initiate cases in the royal courts, and in the maintenance of a permanent archive to keep records of legal facts so that they did not have to be proven in court over and over again.

The writing craft and its paraphernalia, tricks and customs has been a fertile source of strange legal terminology; a sample follows.

Terminology

abstract of title [LE] a summary of the evidences of ownership of real estate, "drawn out (*abs* + *tractum*)" of the official record.

ad sectam, ads. [L] "at the suit of", a way of linking the names of parties in the title of a lawsuit when the defendant's name comes first, useful for indexing the records. If Doe is plaintiff against Smith, the case can be titled Doe *versus* [*vs.* or *v.*] Smith, or else Smith *ad sectam* [*ads.*] Doe.

allonge [LFE] "lengthening", a sheet securely attached to a negotiable instrument to receive endorsements. The attachment must be permanent and tamper-proof to validate the endorsements.

attest [LFE] "to bear witness to (Latin *ad* + *testare*)", especially to declare the validity of a document and its signatures and seals, as a notary public now does, or to verify the truth and accuracy of a copy from the record, as a record clerk does.

cancel [LE] to nullify a record by defacing it with a diagonal grid of pen-strokes like a metal lattice or "chancel". Cf. **chancery** in chapter 14.

certiorari [L] a prerogative writ addressed to a lower court, demanding that the record of a lawsuit there "be made more certain": a writ for judicial review.

charter [HLFE] from the Greek *karta*, then the Latin *carta*, a sheet of Egyptian papyrus for writing. The word was later used to include parchment, then paper, and it reappears in the English **card**. This became the name for a constitution, among persons who knew what it was made of physically but could not read it, as in the case of *Magna Carta*.

codicil [LE] from the Latin *codex,* "book", a written addition to a will that modifies it without harming its validity.

control [LFE] "[to check] against the roll (Latin *contra rotulum*)". This word is now in common use meaning "to govern", "to curb", "to direct another's actions"; it still means also to watch over financial operations and accounts as a **controller** (old spelling **comptroller**) does. The original **control** was the daily work of a clerk of the Pipe Rolls of the English Exchequer, who compared the sheriffs' collections "against the roll", the record of what was owed. Similarly, a person is "brought to book", made to account for himself, after the ceremony in the Exchequer of comparing the sheriff's tallies with the requirements of Domesday Book.

copy [LE] from the Latin *copia*, "full stock", "the whole thing", a rehearsal, verbatim and complete, of a document, record, etc.

counterpart [LFE] from the Latin *contra partem*, a copy against which an original can be compared, an attested and simultaneous second instrument, such as a carbon copy.

crier [GFE] the officer whose duty it was to publish the acts of a court to the illiterate by reading them aloud, and to announce summonses. His functions have contracted to ceremonial ones as the expansion of literacy has replaced his work largely by the Legal Notices in the newspaper. The etymology of the word **cry** leads back to pre-republican Rome. *Quirites* was the collective name for Roman citizens used in the context of public exhortation and protest. An orator would use it to rally his audience against illegalities in high places, and a citizen beset by robbers at night would shout "Quirites!" as a call for help. The verb *quiritare* appeared with the meaning "to shout protest"; passing through the French as *crier*, it appeared in Middle English, paired with the Norman hunting yell *huy*, in **hue and cry**. This was the way a group of townspeople or a crowd at a fair could keep a thief from escaping by pointing and shouting "stop thief!" until he could be run down. The civic obligation to give the **hue-and-cry** was imposed under pain of fines.

culprit [LF] This is a word by mistake: *cul.prit.* was the customary abbreviation, by the clerk of court, of the crown prosecutor's reply joining issue to a plea of not guilty: *Il est **culpable**, je suis **pret***, or in Latin *Culpabilis est, prestus sum*: "He is guilty, and I am ready to proceed to trial." When the judge then addressed the prisoner, he used the note, saying "Culprit, how will you be tried?", and so it seemed to mean "prisoner at the bar."

deed [GE] from Old English *daed*, "act". This word, meaning a written document, indicates that the writing is secondary, merely a record of a thing visibly done, e.g. a ritual delivery of seisin, an entry into real property, a gift, etc.

docket [GE] from Old High German *dokka*, "sheaf", "stump", "short form": a series of minutes of cases in a court, on which notes of their progress and disposition could be made.

document [LE] from the Latin *docere*, "to teach"; "something to teach with", a piece of evidence that shows a fact; hence a **record**.

file [LE] "string", the old way of keeping sheets handy for reference. They were hung on a horizontal cord, either strung on it to be processed in order or hooked on it for ready retrieval. **Patents** could be hung on the file by their pendant seals until claimed by the petitioners.

hand and seal [GE,LFE] This phrase at the end of an instrument is a relic of the ceremony of executing any document when some of the makers or witnesses were illiterate. They would have to touch the parchment, leaving a cross mark as evidence of having done so, and as a religious guarantee of their veracity. Then they would impress their personal seals, using a signet ring, on a circle of wax, and finally the clerk would write in the appropriate name. Cf. **signature** below.

holograph [HE] from the Greek *holo-*, "whole" and *graphein*, "to write"; a letter, will, etc. "written in full" by its author; this word is a Renaissance adoption into English (though Alderman, p. 1117, seems to consider it French).

impanel [LFE] "[to write] on a poster"; a *panel* is a notice board for a public list, especially of a jury.

indenture [LE] from the Latin *dentes*, "teeth"; "toothing action", the jagged cutting between two **counterparts** written on the same sheet, so that each of them will serve to demonstrate the validity of the other. So, a contract drawn in counterpart because it binds both parties, e.g. the kind of contract, for a term of service in exchange for passage, that helped populate the American colonies with "indentured servants". There is a fiction, suggested by this word, that illiterate parties once sealed documents by biting them and leaving a characteristic toothprint.

in forma pauperis [L] "in pauper's form", an abbreviation of court documents and records granted to a poor petitioner; or "without court costs".

in re [L] "in the matter of", the beginning of a court document's title. Not short for "in reference to". The single word *re* means the same as *in re*.

instrument [LE] from the Latin *instruere*, "to make ready"; "equipment", "tool", hence a writing with a practical function and a legal consequence.

locus sigilli, l. s. [L] "place of the seal", an indication on a printed legal form where the maker should impress his signet.

notary public [LE] Shorthand symbols, *notae* in Latin, were a part of the special professional skill of the public legal reporters in ancient Rome; literacy was widespread there, but writing rapidly for courts and contracts required special training and practice in the *notae*. The licensing of legal reporters, *notarii publici*, was revived in the Middle Ages, when their skills had to include legal drafting and letter-writing for a non-literate public.

of record [LE] This phrase reflects the legal importance of public archives, deposits of documents secure enough that they can be used as evidence by themselves. A "matter of record" does not have to be proven by the testimony of the witnesses of the original documents.

patent [LE] "lying open (*patens*)", short for "letters patent", an official letter bearing the seal of a public authority, but not closed by the seal; its contents are public knowledge, and the seal is permanent. The opposite was **letter close**, a secret letter with a seal that could only be broken once.

presents [L>E] short for **these present letters**, "the document you are reading".

record [LFE] "to remember (Latin *recordari*)", and as a noun, "memory".

roll [LE] from *rotulus*, a "little round book", an early Germanic borrowing from Latin, meaning the normal form of an ancient book, whose sheets were glued edge to edge in a row and rolled up for storage: a **volume**. The English Public Records began (ca. 1130) as collections of rolls, each new entry being sewed onto the outside. Some grew so large that they now have to be carried out for consultation in wheelbarrows.

signature [LE] "making a sign (*signum*)", at first meaning either the impression of a signet ring or the very fancy freehand design which a particular notary used to mark his own work: his **sign-manual**. Our custom of assuming that one's own handwriting of one's own name is distinctive enough to guard against fraud comes from the latter practice.

specialty [LFE] from the Latin *speciale*, "particular"; a contract or instrument of debt under seal, not requiring consideration (q.v. in chapter 5).

ss and **SS** The dictionaries consulted either are baffled by this abbreviation or consider it a contraction of *scilicet* (see *viz.* below), which it cannot be. My guess is that it is an abbreviation for *scitum sit* "be it known". The fact that this symbol often appears in capital letters run together hints at an imitation of the golden chain of office (originally the livery sign of the House of Lancaster) worn by the Chancellor and other major ministers of the English crown, and called the **Collar of Esses**. It can be seen in the Holbein portrait of Sir Thomas More.

viz. [L] This is another non-word created by scribes. The Latin words *scilicet* and *videlicet*, "you know" and "you see" were used interchangeably where we in writing English would use a colon (:), "that is", "namely". These frequently used words were abbreviated to look like **scz** and **viz.** The latter, with a rough Old English translation, still appears in many formulas: **viz. to wit.**

Chapter Fourteen

History IV: English Common Law

To get at the historical roots of English Common Law, it is necessary to cut through some mistaken usage. First of all, this was not the customary law of the English common people. Common Law only began to have that connotation in the 16th century, when Lord Chief Justice Coke made a stand on its principles against royal prerogative. Further, it is easy but confusing to use the phrase "Common Law" interchangeably with "British Law". As we have seen, the legal tradition of Great Britain is a compound including Roman Civil Law, Canon Law and Law Merchant as well as Common Law, and the Statutes, whether royal or parliamentary in origin, are not parts of Common Law either. English Common Law was so named because it was the same royal law, common to all parts of the kingdom. It began as a very modest system, offering justice to correct certain very particular abuses in feudal real estate.

The Norman kings of England were, by right of conquest in 1066, overlords of all the land. The feudal tenants of the land all belonged to a pyramid, at the top of which stood the king. Like any feudal lord, the king was responsible for giving justice to his noble vassals and for settling their quarrels. On the other hand, as King of England he had the same rights and responsibilities as the Anglo-Saxon kings had had before the conquest, for criminal justice over all his subjects. Neither role — feudal overlord or king of the country — gave him the right to make law! Norman Feudal Law and English Law were both customary heritages which the king could enforce but could not change.

Knightly society in its original state was based on each knight's capacity to kill and rob. Feudal custom permitted certain kinds of behavior, including land-grabbing by acts of force, which militated against the peace of the kingdom and were probably criminal by Anglo-Saxon law. But the early Norman kings hesitated and failed to enforce on their fellow conquerors the law of the conquered nation, and the result was The Anarchy, as the reign of King Stephen (1135-1154) was nicknamed. It was the brilliant and energetic Henry II (1154-1189) who found a judicial way to repress disorderly self-help with royal law and order.

Henry II inherited considerable land of his own from his royal ancestors: there were royal estates in each shire or county of England, which were managed for him by his reeves or stewards. One reeve for each shire (sheriff) collected and paid into the royal treasury all the dues for the shire: the profits from the royal estates and the "aids" or feudal taxes. The sheriffs were loyal servants of the king; they knew the landholders of the shire, they had armed forces at their disposal, and they had clerks who could read Latin and keep records. The sheriffs were the key to the problem of national justice. As part of his criminal-justice reform, by the Assize of Clarendon (1166) Henry II began sending his Itinerant Justices on circuits (called Eyres, [LF] for "travels") around the kingdom and ordering his sheriffs to empanel "juries of present-ment" to indict the felons of each county. His idea was to give the English frequent opportunities to rid themselves of the murderers, robbers and burglars of their neighborhoods by set-ting the king's own justice upon them. The treasury would get the wealth of those condemned, the peace of the countryside would be improved, and loyalty to the crown would increase.

In the same year (1166), the king began offering easy access to those same Justices in Eyre for anyone who had been robbed of the use of their land, by having his Chancery issue a Writ of

Novel Disseisin on demand. He was acting on the presumption that whenever one knight robbed another of his land, the opinion of the neighborhood would be against the bully and in favor of stability and peace. The uniform Writ of Novel Disseisin stated that, according to the plaintiff, some person had recently deprived him of a piece of land in a particular place. Then it ordered the sheriff to empanel (list) twelve men from that place for a petit jury, and to collect pledges from the plaintiff, defendant, and jury to secure their appearances before the Justices on their next Eyre. When the sheriff brought the case to the Assizes, the jury would be asked whether the plea was true or not, and if their verdict was "true", the sheriff would see to it that the plaintiff recovered possession. Note that the king issued no legislation, but only orders to his servants; that the writ made no mention of "right" but only of fact; and that the feudal tenants on both sides were getting justice in the court of their feudal overlord, not submitting to the law of the commoners. Apart from the proper names, all Writs of Novel Disseisin were the same. The Chancery could scribble them off by the hundred, and these small scrolls with their royal seals were readily recognizable, ubiquitous little emblems of the king's authority. Novel Disseisin was followed by other "original writs", so called because they began lawsuits: Mort d'Ancestor (for an heir to take up inherited land), Utrum (to decide whether a particular piece of land was church land or not), and Darrein Presentment (for the privilege of appointing the holder of a church benefice).

The mass-produced writs and the subsequent assizes were designed to be as cheap, efficient and reliable as possible, but the price was rigidity: the only wrongs which could be righted were those that conformed to the details of the standard writs. The Chancery tried to add flexibility by inventing more writs, notably the very fertile Trespass, but it was caught in the dilemma of standardization *versus* adaptation to particular needs. The judges permitted some leeway and some fictions, allowing a writ to be used successfully when the facts of the case were not quite those of the writ. One judge would follow the example of his predecessors, the lawyers carefully observed the judges, and the gradual develop-

ment of the law by judicial precedent, *stare decisis*, constituted
the history of Common Law for the next seven centuries. Where
Common Law was still too rigid to give justice, Equity came into
service (see Chapter 17).

Further Reading

Theodore Plucknett's *Concise History of the Common Law* (5th
ed., 1956) is the best one-volume survey of English law, not limited
to common law in the strictest sense. The origins and tradition
of the Writs are fully explained in F. W. Maitland's lectures on
The Forms of Action at Common Law (1936). The pioneer judicial
work is described in the fine biography *Henry II* by W. L. Warren
(1973), especially the chapter "Royal Justice", pp. 317-361. For
a revelation of English legal culture at the time when the old
systems were at their most complex and corrupt, see William
Holdsworth's lectures on *Charles Dickens as a Legal Historian*
(1928).

Terminology

assize [LFE] from the Latin *ad* + *sessio*, "a sitting", a meeting
of the English royal council and an ordinance passed at one; a
sitting of a court. Also a meeting of a local council to establish
the weights and measures of local markets, and so **size**.

chancellor [LFE] a secretary stationed at a chancel, the grille
dividing a prince's private chambers from public space; an English

officer of state.

chancery [LFE] the Chancellor's office, then court; the English royal writing office.

circuit court [LFE] a court, under a judge with a royal commission, which traveled by a regular route, meeting in each venue at the same time each year.

common law [LE,NE] in England, the law of royal writs, **common** to the whole country regardless of local custom.

coroner [LE] in medieval England, a local officer charged with prosecuting crown (*corona*) pleas, the practical equivalent of the modern-day American District Attorney, the Canadian Crown Attorney, or the British Director of Public Prosecutions. Since murder was the most important of the crown pleas, the coroner's inquest into the cause of death became his most characteristic activity, and the office is now practically equivalent to, and sometimes called, **medical examiner**.

deem [GE] "to speak judgement"; **doom** is the judgement, **doomsday** the Judgement Day of Christian expectation, and *Domesday Book* the popular name for William the Conqueror's national register of the landed wealth of each county.

disseisin [GFE] "a putting out of possession [of land]". This was the focus of the very first writ of the Common Law, the **Assize of Novel Disseisin**.

grand jury [LFE] or Presentment Jury: a body of men of a county, assembled first in the 12th century to accuse their felonious neighbors under oath, and so to send them before the royal justices for trial.

ignoramus [L] "we do not know", one possible return by a grand jury on an indictment, if the members of the jury find insufficient evidence for a true bill. Ignoramus was also the protagonist and the title of a 17th-century satirical comedy in which the Civil Law students at Cambridge University made fun of the Common Lawyers and ridiculed their poor Latin.

nisi prius [L] "unless earlier …". A writ from the early 13th century that allowed a petitioner to finish his case and get a settlement from the Court of King's Bench stationed at Westminster Palace, "**unless, earlier,** the justices shall have come to the county." It would be more convenient for everybody to finish the trial under the circuit judges in the county sessions. The name *nisi prius* got attached to the circuit courts that judged private lawsuits with a jury, and loosely to any court of first instance with judge and jury. See a **nisi prius lawyer** in chapter 19.

petit jury [LFE] "small jury", limited to twelve. From the 12th century on, such juries were empanelled by the sheriff to give their verdict in answer to a Common Law writ. From the 13th century on, they were also authorized to give criminal verdicts in cases following from grand jury indictments.

praecipe [L] "Command!", a writ, addressed to the sheriff, ordering him to issue an order; such a writ would permit, as an alternative to compliance, that the person ordered might appear in court to show cause why he should not comply.

seisin [GE] "holding", real possession.

serjeant [LFE] the French version of the Latin *serviens*, "someone serving" in one of several official capacities, variously spelled, e.g. a sergeant-at-arms or serjeant-at-law.

sheriff [GE] "shire-reeve", the royal steward for a whole county, responsible for collecting and paying to the Exchequer the revenues of the royal properties there, and (while he was about it) administering justice by the Common Law writs.

solicitor [LFE] from the Latin *sollicitus*, "anxious"; "one who takes care", in England a qualified and licensed legal agent who watches over the clients' rights and legal activities in general, but does not appear for them in court; for that purpose the solicitor will **brief** (q.v. in Chapter 3) a trial attorney or barrister, so called because he appears at the bar of the court.

special pleading   This phrase, with its modern meaning of tricky ex-parte argument, was used from the late 17th century to refer to the practice of arguing particular cases into conformity with the common-law writs and accepted legal fictions, and into direct conflict (issue) with the adverse party, a legal art so complicated that it was performed by a sub-class of lawyers called special pleaders.

tales [L] When a petit jury had lost members due to challenges or other causes, the sheriff was empowered to bring it up to strength by choosing enough *tales de circumstantibus*, "**the same sort** of men from the bystanders", persons qualified in the same way as the original jury. One so chosen is called a **talesman**.

Ubi jus, ibi remedium   [L] "Where there is a right, there is a remedy". The discussion in Broom (pp. 191-211) attributes the growth of Common Law actions into contractual liability to this principle.

verdict [LFE] "something told truly (Latin *vere dictum*)", the jury's conclusion. Note that originally the juries were expected to come to court already knowing the necessary facts.

voir dire [LF] "to tell the truth", the pre-examination of a juror or witness under oath. Not "to see speaking", as Alderman (p. 1120) believed.

writ [GE] "something written", especially one of the small, highly recognizable Common-Law orders to the sheriff.

Chapter Fifteen

Real Property

When Duke William of Normandy backed up his questionable legal claim to the crown of England by his invasion of the island in 1066, his army was made up of knights, mounted warriors of the feudal ruling class of Normandy. After the conquest was complete, England was parceled out to the invaders as fiefs, i.e. feudal tenements. Landholding in medieval England was therefore 1) originally by right of conquest, 2) passed by heredity, 3) one of the chief legal interests and problems of the king and nobility, and 4) a matter discussed and litigated in French. In more modern times, the land law has had to take into account the possibility of buying and selling land, and the many kinds of rights or **estates** that may exist in land. To deal with these problems, it was necessary to adopt some Civil Law categories and language.

Terminology

a coelo usque ad centrum [L] "from heaven to the center [of the earth]", the vertical extent of land ownership in Civil Law. Note the presumption of a spherical earth.

ab antiquo [L] "from old times".

abandon [FE] The French *a bandon* meant "into the power", and the verb *abandonner* "to surrender"; to give up control or possession.

abeyance [FE] from the Old French *baer*, "to yawn"; "gaping after", the condition of a land right which is waiting for the law to decide ownership. The emptiness of a title.

aboriginal [LE] "from the beginning (*ab origine*)", as the European colonists presumed were the land titles of the native inhabitants of America, etc.

abut [FE] "to meet back to back (Old French *a* + *but*)", said of lands bordering each other.

access [LE] from the Latin *accessus*, "means of approach".

accession [LFE] from the Latin *ad* + *cessio*, "addition"; or "coming into [a property or dignity]".

accretion [LFE] from the Latin *ad* + *crescere*, "to grow on to"; accumulation, as of land by river deposits.

adhesion contract [LE] a contract that really binds (*ad* + *haesit*) only one side, now usually presented as a printed form by the other.

adverse possession [LE] from the Latin *ad* + *versus*, "turned against"; possession maintained against other possible interests for a period long enough to secure legal title; other persons with claims lose them by **laches**, q.v. in chapter 17; cf. **prescription** below, and **squatter's rights** in chapter 19.

alien [LFE] an adjective meaning "another's"; or a verb meaning "to transfer to another", also found in the direct Latin derivation **alienate**.

alluvion [LE] soil deposited by water that flows (*alluit*), a special problem in real estate.

ancient lights [LFE,GFE] "old windows", a right, attached to a particular real property, not to be shaded by new buildings or plantings. Now usually part of "air rights".

animus manendi [L] "intention to remain", a characteristic of a person in domicile.

appurtenance [LFE] "[a thing] belonging to (Latin *ad* + *pertinens*) [another thing]", as a fixture to land, one right to another right, etc.

blackacre, whiteacre [GE] fictitious names of properties used as examples in cases or form books.

condominium [LE] from the Latin *con* + *dominus*; "joint lordship", now chiefly refers to landlordship, but once applied to any lordly right, e.g. justice, when shared by several lords.

conveyance [LFE] "carrying over (Latin *con* + *vehens*)", the whole process of transfer of a title, including the necessary new entries on the record.

cum onere [L] "with the burden", subject to a charge; e.g. the transfer of a property with a mortgage on it.

demise [LFE] from the Latin *de* + *missum*, the French *de* + *mise*, "a giving over", a noun meaning "conveyance" or a verb meaning "to convey".

domicile [LE] from the Latin *domus*, "home"; legal place of residence.

dominant tenement [LE] a landholding to which another landholding has a **servitude** q.v. below.

easement [FE] "giving of ease", accommodation, especially the use of property not one's own. Now usually claimed by public utilities, to place their lines or pipes on private property.

ejectment [LFE] "throwing out (Latin *e* + *jectum*)", as an act of private force, or as execution of a court order.

emphyteusis [HLE] from the Greek *em* + *phyteusis*, "engrafting", the work of a gardener or vine-dresser; a hereditary or long-term right to the lease of another's land, originally on condition that the tenant would cultivate it.

encroachment [FE] from the French *croche* "a hook"; "putting a hook into", a gradual intrusion on another's property or rights.

encumbrance [FE] from the French *combre*, "log"; the burdening of a property with a debt or **servitude**, q.v. below.

entry [LFE] from the Late Latin *intrare*, "to go in" or "to put in"; a putting into the record; or the peaceful assumption of possession of a property by walking into it.

escheat [LFE] from the Latin *ex* + *cadere*; "falling out", the reversion of land, once to the lord, now to the state, when heritage fails.

escrow [GFE] from the Old High German *scrot*, "fragment"; "a scroll", as a deed or property held by a third party until full payment is made for land, then delivered to the purchaser.

estate [LFE] from the Latin *status*, "standing"; "condition"; the precise interest a person has in a real property; also, the collective property, personal and real, of a decedent person.

estovers [LFE] the consumptions of property for necessities allowed by law, e.g. cutting timber for building repairs. The Latin *est opus*, "it is necessary", became the French *estovoir*.

farm [GE+LFE] This word combines meanings taken from the Anglo-Saxon *feorm* meaning "food" and the Latin *firmum* meaning "steady": an agricultural property with a fixed-rent lease.

fee simple [GFE,LE] a full and free fief or estate in land, whereas **fee tail** [GFE,FE] is a "cut fief", an estate limited as to who can inherit it, and an inalienable one. Note that the old name for a vassal's property in feudal tenure under a lord is **fief**, a noun; and that "fiefdom" is pseudo-antiquary silliness.

fixture [LE] from the Latin *fixus*, "established"; "something attached", as a building to land or a door to a house, and so legally part of it.

foreclosure [LFE] from the Latin *clausum*, "shut", with the Old English *fore*, "earlier"; the ending of a mortgagor's right of redemption before he exercises it.

freehold [GE] an estate for life or in fee.

inure [LFE] from the Latin *in* + *utere*, "to come into use", to take effect.

lease [LFE] from the Latin *laxare*, "to loosen", through the French *laisser*; a contract to allow another to occupy a tenement, not permanently.

lien [LFE] from the Latin *ligamen*, "a link"; the right to hold a real property until a debt is satisfied; e.g. a "mechanic's lien" on a house is held by a carpenter until he is paid for his repairs to the house.

metes and bounds [LFE] "measures and terminal points", given in the written description of a property. The Latin phrase in the records is *per metas et bundas*. *Meta* is ancient Latin for "measure", while *butina*, "boundary" is a Late Latin adoption, possibly from German because it appears in a Latin version of the laws of the Ripuarian Franks.

mortgage [LFE] "dead security" for a loan, consisting of a conveyance of land (see Alderman, p. 1118).

mortmain [LFE] "dead hand", a permanent, inalienable possession, as by a church or other immortal corporation (see Alderman, p. 1118).

Nemo potest plus juris ad alium transferre quam ipse habet. [L] "No one can transfer to another more of right than he has himself"; also found in the short form *Nemo dat quod non habet*, "No one gives what he does not have." *Digest* rule 54, *Sextus* rule 79. Broom (pp. 467-469) gives examples: one who holds land on a lease cannot sell it; one who holds real estate encumbered by a mortgage cannot transfer it free and clear; a joint tenant cannot give a whole estate.

personalty [LFE] movable goods, attached to a person, contrasted with **realty**.

plat [LFE] "flat", a map of record.

premises [LE] "set out in advance (*prae + missa*)", the first statements of a logical argument (see chapter 20) or the first paragraphs of a document. Those of a deed of land give a precise description of the property, including its **metes and bounds**, which is why a building or a field or a mine can be called "the premises."

prescription [LE] "drawing a line around (*prae + scriptio*)": the assertion of a claim to property by real use of it. Related to **adverse possession** and **squatter's rights**.

profit a prendre [F] right to take a share of produce of another's land.

Qui prior est tempore, potior est jure. [L] "He who is earlier in time is stronger in right", *Sextus* rule 54. Broom (pp. 363-365) applies the maxim to right of salvage, stray cattle and other *bona vacantia* which can be possessed by the first finder, and "where there are two conflicting titles, the elder shall be preferred."

quitclaim [LFE] "quieting the cry", ending a claim of possession. A quitclaim deed releases all the grantor's title and rights.

right of way [GE] an easement for passage through another's land.

servitude [LE] the condition of a person or a property bound to serve another: slavery (*servitus*), or a burden such as right of way for the benefit of a neighboring property called the **dominant tenement**, q.v. above.

tenancy [LFE] "holding (Latin *tenens*) [a property]", by whatever title.

tenement [L] "[a property] held".

terminus ad quem [L] "the limit to which", end point of time or place.

terminus a quo [L] "the limit from which", beginning point of time or place.

title [LE] from the Latin *titulus*, "headline", "inscription"; the owner's mark and so (vaguely), "ownership".

warranty deed [GFE] a deed in which the grantor warrants a good and clear title.

Chapter Sixteen

Criminal Procedure

Anglo-American criminal procedure is unlike any past system of assigning responsibility for delinquencies against the common good, on account of two extraneous influences that we usually accept without question: 1) the presumption of innocence and 2) the principle that there is no crime without criminal intent. The first came into criminal procedure as the reciprocal of the English Common Law right of trial by jury; the other is the Judeo-Christian religious notion, transmitted to us by Canon Law, that sin or crime is essentially a mental act, an act of will, before it becomes overt and physical.

We saw (in the introduction to chapter 14) how King Henry II took control of a national pattern of real-estate usurpations by opening his courts to all petitioners with the possessory writs beginning in 1166. In the same year, he moved aggressively against the customary-law crimes of murder, robbery and theft by having his sheriffs empanel "juries of presentment", the original Grand Juries, to declare what they knew of crime and criminals in their neighborhoods. When the itinerant justices came around on their circuits, the sheriffs would bring before them all those who had been indicted and arrested, and they would be tried by ordeal, usually the ordeal of cold water. This meant that after pleading innocent, the accused would be bound and dropped into a pond which had been blessed by a priest, and if he sank he would be found innocent (and rescued).

In 1215, the trials by ordeal became impossible because Pope Innocent III, in the Fourth Lateran Council, forbade the clergy to bless them. It had been too much like summoning God to do the work of the courts. Then the royal justices were forced to have the indictments, plus some evidence, laid before petit juries, sometimes the same juries that had been empaneled to give verdicts on the possessory writs. From this makeshift solution developed the tradition of criminal trial by jury.

Terminology

accusation [LE] "the bringing of a cause against (*ad + causa*) someone".

acquit [LFE] "to quiet [a complaint] toward someone"; the noun is **acquittal**.

admission [LE] from the Latin *ad + missum*, "giving in"; a confession of guilt; or the ruling that certain evidence may be introduced in a trial; also a judge's acceptance of bail for discharge of a prisoner.

alias [L] "otherwise", usually used to introduce an alternative name for a person.

amnesty [HLE] from the Greek *a + mnestia*, "lack of memory", "forgetting"; the nullification of a criminal offense by the sovereign power.

arraign [LFE] The Latin *ad rationem* meant either "at the rate of", in which case it was and is abbreviated "@", or "to an explanation". The Old French verb *arainer* meant "to call to account". In Anglo-American criminal procedure, the **arraignment** is the formal ceremony of reading the **indictment** or **information** (q.v. below) and demanding the prisoner's plea.

attainder [LFE] "a tainting", the civil death that followed a capital sentence of felony. A bill of attainder could condemn a person without trial, and was prohibited by the U.S. Constitution 1.9.

autopsy [HE] "seeing for oneself (*auto* + *opsia*)", a post-mortem anatomical examination to determine the cause of death and whether or not it was criminally caused.

autrefois acquit, autrefois convict [F] "acquitted another time", "convicted another time", the criminal application, in Law French, of the maxim *Res judicata* ..., q.v. in chapter 6.

bail [LFE] from the Latin *bajulus*, "porter"; "something delivered [as security]"; see **bailiff** in chapter 6. **Bail** is a deposit of valuable security with the clerk of court against the appearance of the accused. The word also appears in contracts, meaning security for performance, delivered in an act called **bailment** by a **bailor** to a **bailee**.

bench warrant [GFE] a process, e.g. for contempt, issued by a trial judge.

capias [L] "you should seize [a person]"; a writ for arrest, specifically *capias ad respondendum*, the most common one, "... to answer [a charge]" and *capias ad satisfaciendum*, "... to satisfy [damages which have been awarded]".

compounding a felony [LFE] **Compound** and its derivatives are derived from the Latin *componere*, "to bring together", "settle a dispute". **Compounding** or *compositio* by a medieval law officer or private party referred to "composing" or legitimately settling a complaint by accepting a sum of money, out of court or as part of a judicial proceeding. Today the phrase carries the other connotation of "compound", "to add on", and seems to mean making a felony worse by concealing it or failing to prosecute it.

confession [LE] from the Latin *con* + *fessus*, "said completely"; "a declaration" of specific guilt.

confession and avoidance [LE,LFE] a plea that admits the fact of a charge, and then gives grounds to nullify it.

conviction [LE] "total defeat".

discovery [LFE] from the Latin *dis* + *cooperire*, "uncovering", "revealing": pre-trial motions to ascertain the adversary's case in order to meet it.

disposition [LFE] "placement", the final settlement of a criminal case, sentence, discharge, or other.

examination [LE] "weighing in a pair of scales (*examina*)", a trial of evidence, later the process of eliciting testimony from witnesses in a trial.

exculpate [LE] "to take [a person or oneself] out of guilt (*culpa*)", to plead an excuse or justification (especially if successful).

ex relatione, ex rel. [L] "from the relation of", a phrase in the title of a criminal record introducing the name of the person who laid the information which began the prosecution.

guilty [GEFE] *gylt*, the Old English for "fault", transformed into the Law French *guilté* and back into English.

habeas corpus [L] "you should have the body", a writ to bring a prisoner out of prison for trial or release. The phrase therefore stands for the traditional Anglo-American civil right of freedom from unjust or capricious imprisonment, implicit in Magna Carta and explicitly legislated in the Habeas Corpus Act of 1680.

Ignorantia facti excusat, ignorantia juris non excusat. [L] "Ignorance of a fact is an excuse; ignorance of the law is not." *Liber*

Sextus rule 13, fully discussed by Broom, pp. 253-267.

indictment [LFE] "a declaration". This peculiar word, once spelled **indite** until the *c* was put back in from the Latin *dictare*, "to state", means the return of a true bill by a grand jury against a person accused, sending him to trial.

information [LE] an official's "giving shape (*forma*)" to a court's knowledge of crime; a criminal charge leading to trial without the action of a grand jury.

insanity [LE] "unhealthiness", usually referring, even in classical times, to mental illness. A cause of reduced criminal capacity.

marshal [GFE] from the Old High German *marahscalc*, "horse tender", a royal court's cavalry professional, and a high officer of state in England. The Earl Marshall was responsible for keeping order in the royal court and central lawcourts, and a judge on circuit was guarded by his own marshal. In the U.S., a marshal is an officer in charge of protecting the courts and executing their orders.

mistrial [L/GFE] "wrong trial", invalid or incomplete.

modus operandi [L] "way of working" (plural *modi operandi*), a method of criminal activity which might be argued in court as characteristic of the accused and so as evidence against him.

nolo contendere [L] "I do not wish to contest it", a plea used in the US with the legal effect of a guilty plea, except that civil suits cannot be based on the consequent conviction.

post mortem [L] "[examination] after death".

presentment [LFE] "a laying [of information] before (Latin *praesentare*)": a grand jury's notice of crime without indictment.

quash [LFE] The Late Latin *cassare* meant "to overthrow"; **quash** is now used especially of an indictment.

remand [LE] "to order back (*re* + *mandare*)" a prisoner into custody after a **habeas corpus** (q.v. above) hearing; or to order a case back to the court that heard it, after an appellate hearing.

sentence [LE] "opinion (*sententia*)", the formal settlement by a judge, and its exact wording. Now restricted to criminal decisions, while **judgement** and **award** are used for civil ones.

subornation of perjury [LE,LFE] "secretly to arrange (Latin *sub* + *ordinare*) a perjury".

summary [LE] restricted to the "high points (*summa*)" in a quick judicial procedure.

summons [LFE] an order to come to court, "with a warning attached (Latin *sub* + *monere*)", equivalent to the Civil Law citation. See Millar, p. 1025.

venire facias [L] "you should cause [a jury] to come", a writ to a sheriff to empanel a jury from the county or a smaller area. The list or **panel** of jurors is sometimes called the **venire**, and the place they represent the **venue**. When there is a public excitement against the accused, a change of venue — a trial elsewhere with a jury of strangers — might be granted.

Chapter Seventeen

Equity

Aequitas quasi aequalitas, goes an old maxim: "Equity is a sort of equality", an evenhanded fairness. In short, equity is the most general kind of justice, free to step beyond the formal limitations of law. With the development and solidification — amounting almost to petrifaction — of the English Common Law, the system retained its flexibility and capacity to handle new kinds of problems through the equity courts operated by the different departments of the central government, such as the Admiralty and the Exchequer. The Chancery was in a special position. It was the office which produced the writs of Common Law, and, representing as it did the boundless capacity of the King to give justice, it could make up new writs for courts to hear new kinds of cases. It could also reserve cases for the Chancellor to hear, without a Common Law writ, by equity.

Equity in England "followed the law" where possible, and supplemented it with rules drawn from other and older legal traditions, such as the Maxims derived from Civil and Canon Rules of Law. But the Court of Chancery eventually became bogged down in its own rules of procedure and its record-worship, and there was no superior department to rescue it. Charles Dickens, who lost a bundle of money in the course of winning the *Christmas Carol* copyright case in Chancery, considered the court a disgrace to the name of Equity, and he pilloried it in his novel *Bleak House*, especially the first chapter, one of the finest passages of prose ever written about the law.

Separate Equity jurisdictions in North America were gradually merged into the courts of law, a process that was not fully complete until New Jersey abolished its separate equity system in 1947.

A brief word about the Maxims. They are mostly in Latin, which is ironic because the Roman jurisconsults frowned on any attempt to put their law into nutshells. In the last title of the *Digest*, Justinian's committee reluctantly recognized the usefulness of 211 "rules of ancient law", and at the end of the 13th century Pope Boniface VIII published 88 "Rules of Law" at the end of the *Liber Sextus*. English lawyers felt free to make use of these foreign rules, but not exactly as rules. When arguing in equity, they would refer to the Civil and Canon Law materials as witnesses to natural justice, and use the rules as most general or largest logical premises: **maxima** (cf. chapter 20). The history of the maxims in jurisprudence is explained by Peter Stein, *Regulae juris* (1966).

Terminology

admiralty [AF+LE] The Arabic title of the Saracen "commander of the sea" was *amir-al-bar*, adopted in French and confused with the obvious Latin *admirabilis* into admiral. In England the Admiralty, like other high offices of state, was also a court, one with expertise on naval matters at its disposal; it was used as a court of equity in maritime matters and international trade.

Aequitas sequitur legem. [L] "Equity follows the law", i.e. applies legal rules wherever possible, and acts only after law has failed to give justice.

arbitration [LE] The Latin word *arbiter* meant a very informal bystander or onlooker, then a decider of cases with wider powers than a *judex*. As we use it, **arbitration** is the deciding of a dispute by an umpire satisfactory to both sides, when both have agreed to abide by the decision.

bill in equity [GE,LE] the initial pleading in equity; see Millar pp. 1025-1026 for the derivation from *libellus*.

cease and desist [LFE] an administrative order like a court **injunction**, q.v. below. The words are practically synonymous, and pairing them is a habit of legal language, partly a heritage from the oral customary law tradition. For more examples, see Mellinkoff, pp. 121-122.

cestui que [F] "the one who", used in phrases to identify the various persons in a trust: *cestui que trust*, "the one who trusts", is the beneficiary; so is *cestui que use*, but only of usufruct; *cestui que vie*, "the one who does the living", is the person whose lifetime is the duration of the trust.

clean hands [GE] innocence, freedom from inequity. The doctrine is expressed, "He who comes to equity must come with clean hands".

construction [LE] understanding of language in context, the building of the legal meanings of words. The verb is **to construe**, derived like the noun and the following adjective from the Latin *construere*, "to build".

constructive [LE] "established by [the court's] construing [of a document or a set of facts]," in contrast to **explicit** or actual.

contra bonos mores [L] "against good customs", "against good morals".

cy pres [LF] "near to it", a rule of the equitable construction of documents that aims as near as possible to the intention of the maker, if that intent itself was illegal or impossible.

decree [LF] "something decided (*decretum*)", once a law, especially an ecclesiastical one; now an order of a court of equity, equivalent to a judgement at law; see Millar, p. 1029.

dolus malus [L] "bad fraud", the wrongful kind, intending to deceive for profit. By contrast, "Whoever's calling, tell them I'm out" is a *dolus bonus* or "good fraud". The plurals would be *doli mali* and *doli boni*.

ejusdem generis [L] "of the same kind", the name of a rule of construction, that general words are clarified by specific words in the same context.

equity [LFE] "evenness (Latin *aequitas*)", "fairness", "justice".

estoppel [GFE] a bar to the assertion of one's own right caused by one's own action. For example, if I have sued to collect rent for an apartment, I am **estopped** from pleading that I don't own the place and don't owe the taxes on it. See Fullagar, p. 7.

ethics [HLE] The Greek *ethos* meant a dramatic character and the action appropriate to him; **ethics** is the philosophical study of the behavior correct for a particular station or occupation.

ex aequo et bono [L] "out of fairness and goodness", "in equity and conscience".

Expressio unius est exclusio alterius. [L] "The expression of one thing is the exclusion of another". Broom, pp. 651-669, has applications of this rule of construction.

fiduciary [LE] "related to a trust". The *fiduciarius* meant "trustee", and was derived from *fidus*, "faithful", which came in turn from *fides*, "good faith".

gratuitous [LFE] "as a favor (Latin *gratia*)", given without consideration of a benefit in return.

Id certum est quod certum reddi potest. [L] "That is certain which can be made certain". For example, "before Election Day 1990" would serve as a "date certain" for payment on a contract. Broom, pp. 623-626.

implied promise [LFE] a **constructive** promise in contract.

Impossibilium nulla obligatio est. [L] "There is no obligation to impossible things". *Digest* rule 185, *Sextus* rule 6. Broom, pp. 242-252 deals with a variant of this maxim.

in kind [L>E] translates the Latin *in specie*, "specifically" or "specific"; cf. **specific performance** below.

injunction [LE] from the Latin *injungere*, "attach"; "something imposed", a prohibition laid on a defendant in equity. The judge is said to enjoin someone from some action.

laches [LFE] The Latin *laxitas* and then the French *lachesse* meant "looseness", "absence of strain", and so neglect; the delay in asserting a right that allows it to lapse. See the maxim *Vigilantibus* ... below.

law of nations [L>E] translates the Latin *jus gentium*, which used to mean **natural law**, q.v. below, as observed by all peoples, in contrast to the peculiarly Roman Civil Law. Now the meaning is rather "international law".

malpractice [LFE] "bad [professional] function", especially in doctors or lawyers.

natural law [LE,NE] a system of law harmonious with the nature of the world and of humankind, a concept in philosophical jurisprudence. See also **law of nations** above.

Non videntur qui errant consentire. [L] "It seems that persons in error do not consent". Broom, p. 262, says that equity gives relief from losses which are caused by a party's ignorance or mistake in a contract.

Noscitur a sociis. [L] "It is known from its associates". Broom, pp. 588-593: the rule of construction that words are to be understood in their contexts, not in the abstract.

Omnis definitio in jure civili periculosa est. [L] "Every definition in Civil Law is perilous". *Digest* rule 202.

on all fours "in substantial agreement", said of one case in comparison with another, when they differ in no material respect, and the judgement in one can be expected in the other.

quantum meruit [L] "as much as he deserved", an award in case of implied contract of employment; cf. *quantum valebant* above in chapter 5.

quasi [L] "as if", sometimes used as an adjective equivalent to **constructive**, q.v. above.

Quod ab initio non valet, tractu temporis non convalescit. [L] "What is invalid from the beginning does not become valid by the passage of time." This is a variant of *Digest* rule 210, *Sextus* rule 18, applied at length by Broom, pp. 178-183. A fine German paraphrase runs *Hundert Jahr Unrecht wird keine Stunde Recht*: "A century of wrong makes not an hour of right". A prescription founded on fraud or violence does not establish a right.

relief [LFE] from the Latin *re + levare*, "to lift away"; "a lightening", "removal of a burden" by an action in equity.

remedy [LFE] "a cure (Latin *remedium*)" for injustice, a **redress**, q.v. in chapter 21.

replevin [LFE] from the French *plevir*, "to pledge"; "the restoration of a pledge", an action or decree for recovery in kind; the verb is to **replevy**.

specific performance [LE] a remedy, decreeing the fulfillment of a contract in its own terms, not in cash damages.

stale claim [GE,LFE] one that has lost its strength by long dormancy.

trespass [LFE] from the Latin *trans*, "across" and *passus*, "a step"; "to walk through", and as a noun, the act of doing so; illegal entry on another's land or a transgression of law.

trial [L?FE] As Millar (p. 1028) shows, **trial** and the verb to **try** come from an Old French verb *trier*, "to sift", which also gives us **triage**. It is possible that there is a Latin antecedent, a frequentative *tritare* from the verb *terere*, "to grind". The "mills of justice" is an old figure of speech.

trust [NE] from Old Norse *traust*, "good faith", "confidence", so the confiding of a property to one person for the benefit of another who could not manage, defend, or legally own it. The holder in trust is called the **trustee**, and see *cestui* above.

turpitude [LE] from the Latin *turpis*, "filthy"; "dirtiness", wickedness plus bad reputation.

Vigilantibus et non dormientibus jura subveniunt. [L] "The laws assist the vigilant, not the sleeping", the maxim which expresses the doctrine of **laches**, q.v. above. See Broom, pp. 892-903.

waiver [GFE] "abandonment of a waif", "renunciation [of a right]".

words of art [GE,LE] technical words, or words with particular meanings within the language of a particular trade or profession. *Ars* in Latin, like *techne* in Greek, meant a skilled craft.

Chapter Eighteen

Commercial Law

Terminology

account [LFE] The Latin *computare*, "to count up" is the source of this and cognate words in all the Romance languages. Rapid calculating with the abacus and the keeping of double-entry books that could be used as proof in court were developed by international traders and notaries in 13th-century Italy, and wherever the technique spread, the courts had to learn it.

accrue [LFE] "to grow onto", become the property of a person. From the Latin *ad* + *crescere*.

agent [LE] "one acting [for a principal]" under a special or general authorization; see Fullagar, pp. 7-8.

ancillary [LE] "auxiliary", "subordinate"; the Latin *ancilla* meant "a maidservant."

anticipation [LE] from the Latin *ante* + *capere*, "taking before [due]".

auction [LE] "increasing (*auctio*)" the price of goods on sale until only one buyer remains willing to pay it.

authority [LFE] from the Latin *auctor*, "founder", "author"; the full power to dispose of a thing, such as its creator has. This power can be delegated in fractions or degrees to an agent.

bill of lading [LE,GE] **Bill** is from **libel** or *libellus*, a little book. **Lading** is "loading". So, the document that certifies that a carrier has received specified goods. Bills of lading include waybills and airbills.

binder [GE] a temporary document of contract, or receipt for the deposit of earnest money, which begins the operation of the contract.

boycott a concerted refusal to do business with a person or company, named after Charles Boycott, an English rental agent in Ireland (d. 1897) who was so treated because of his economic cruelties.

breach [GFE] "breaking", especially of an agreement or contract.

broker [GFE] one who broaches or taps a barrel, buys in bulk and sells portions; a cargo-breaker, dealer at a port. Note the similar idea in **retail**, "cutting up". Now any businessman who mediates between sellers and buyers.

Caveat emptor. [L] "Let the buyer beware". Broom, pp. 768-809, applies this maxim to the sale of land as well as movables, and finds that the law will not help a careless purchaser, only one who was **warranted** and then disappointed, or who suffered from the seller's fraud.

check, cheque [Persian, AFE] the instrument of a bank draft, and the means of controlling a bank account. The U.S. spelling is check. The Persian word for king, *shah,* was the Arabic word for the game of chess, adopted with the game into French as *eschec*; the English royal court of accounts was named the Exchequer because its counting table was ruled off into squares like a chessboard.

It seems likely that the first commercial-paper **cheques** were Exchequer drafts.

concurrent [LE] "running together (*con* + *currens*)".

consignment [LE] "sealing together", the entrusting of goods to a carrier, and the goods entrusted.

del credere agent [I+LE] a sales agent who also guarantees the credit of the buyer.

demurrage [LFE] "delay", the detention of a ship for loading, and the payment to indemnify the owner for that delay. Cf. **demur** in chapter 3.

disburse [LFE] to pay out of a public or corporate purse (Latin *bursa*) or fund.

disclaimer [LFE] "a crying off (Latin *dis* + *clamare*)", repudiation of a claim, or the denial that one is making a claim.

draft [GFE] from the Old English *dragan*, "to draw"; "a drawing", a withdrawal; or "writing".

factor [LE] "maker": one who makes, and specifically, makes money by selling; a sales agent.

franchise [GFE] from the Old High German *franko*, meaning "a Frank" or "a free man"; "freedom"; a license, e.g. to sell a brand of goods or to vote.

fungible [LE] from the Latin *fungi*, "to serve a purpose"; "serviceable", describes goods as practically interchangeable by measure and count in trade, e.g. crude oil or wheat.

guaranty [GFE] "a guarding", a promise to perform if the principal contractor fails to do so, also the act of promising by a **guarantor** to the other party to the contract, who becomes the **guarantee. Guarantee** is also a variant spelling for **guaranty**. Cf. **warranty** below.

implied [LFE] "folded in (Latin *implicatum*)", as the authority to issue receipts is **implied** in the authority to sell, or a warranty of merchantability is implied by an offer to sell.

indorse [LFE] "[write] on the back (Latin *in* + *dorsum*)", a conventional way to discharge one's own possession of a negotiable instrument such as a check. Also spelled **endorse**.

interest [LE] Latin for "the difference is ...", any premium for a loan, the difference between what is lent and what is repaid: usury in the old sense, q.v. in chapter 5.

interference [LE] "carrying oneself in between [parties]", or the invasion of a patent right by another patent.

laissez faire [F] "let it work", a principle of the political economy of Adam Smith and others, that the government should not interfere in the market.

legal tender [LE,LFE] a legal "holding forth (Latin *tendere*, Old French *tendre*)", an offering of value that is legally proper to pay a debt, especially current money. **Tender** with the meaning "soft, delicate" is also *tendre* in Old French, but is derived from the Latin *tener*.

license [LE] "permission" by a public authority or a corporation for a person to use public or corporate powers or facilities, e.g. a public road or a patented design. The noun comes from the Latin *licentia,* and in Britain and Canada is spelled **licence.**

merchantability [LFE] "saleability", the basic suitability of goods for the purpose for which they are offered for sale, and the warranty implied by the offer.

mutual [LE] from the Latin *mutuum*, "a change"; "exchanging", "reciprocal", common to the parties.

negotiable instrument [LE] a document of value that can be exchanged.

principal [LE] "taking (*ceps*) the front (*primum*) chair" in an assembly; "leading" or "chief"; the one whose authority an agent uses.

property [LFE] From the Latin *proprietas*, "ownership", belonging to one person. The phrase "public property" is a contradiction in terms, according to the root meanings of the words.

receiver [LFE] a public agent to collect debts due to a bankrupt corporation.

reciprocity [LE] from adverb forms of the Latin *re + pro*, "back and forth"; "mutuality". The condition in which two jurisdictions grant each other similar advantages, or two corporations agree to favor each other as suppliers.

Respondeat superior. [L] "Let the principal answer": Broom, pp. 843-866. Employees, servants, and agents acting within the scope of delegated authority or employment are not liable themselves, but render their employers, masters, or principals liable.

Simplex commendatio non obligat. [L] "Mere praise does not obligate", a rule of the Civil Law (*Digest* 4.3.37). The sign reading "Good Used Cars" is a mere puffing of the goods, not a warranty, however brightly lit.

tariff [AIE] The Arabic *ta'rif* meant "a public notice", in particular a schedule of duties on imports and exports, and by extension a schedule of freight rates or other charges listed in a public notice.

transaction [LE] "acting across", a dealing between persons that changes their legal relations, including contracts.

transfer [LE] "to carry over", or the act of carrying over.

underwrite [GE] to insure or guaranty, once done by a clause literally subscribed to a contract of sale or shipping by the insurer.

usage [LFE] custom, especially of trade.

vicarious [LFE] "by a stand-in", "through an agent".

warranty [GFE] This doublet of **guaranty** and **warrant** means a representation by a seller as to the quality of the goods being sold, a part of the sale contract, express or implied.

Chapter Nineteen

History V: The North American Reception of European Law

The European settlement of the Americas included the impor-
tation of the major European traditions of law, but not
homogeneously or simultaneously. Colonial Spanish America, including the southeast and southwest of North America, was
governed more or less closely by a Viceroy of the Indies in part-
nership with a strong Catholic Church, and the earliest organized
law of these territories was an extension of the royal and ecclesiastical laws of Spain. To this complex was added the Civil Law
of the Empire when, in 1519, Charles I of Spain, the Habsburg
heir of Ferdinand and Isabella, was elected Holy Roman Emperor.

The French territories of North America, organized under the
mercantile system of Louis XIV and Colbert, were legal exten-
sions of the French metropolis. Their law was the Custom of Paris,
and it depended for its development on legislation and legal precedent in France. The customary law of Quebec was therefore frozen
in 1763, when the province was annexed to the British crown.
Subsequently, the private law of Quebec has largely assimilated
to Napoleon's Civil Code of 1804, itself mostly a Civil restatement of the Custom of Paris. In Louisiana the metropolitan French
legal regime, streaked with Spanish-Habsburg elements, continued
until the United States purchased the Territory in 1803. The Code

Napoleon appeared, therefore, only after Louisiana's political link
with France had been broken, but the Territory voluntarily imi-
tated the French Code in its own Code of 1808, and the Livingston
Code of 1825 matched the Code Napoleon about 80%. And so
it is incorrect but not misleading to refer to both Quebec and Louisiana as observing the Code Napoleon.

Upper Canada (Ontario) and the British colonies on the Atlan-
tic seaboard belong, loosely speaking, to the Common Law tradition. More precisely, the law of English-speaking North America
is a British-style mixture of English Common Law, equitable principles derived from Civil and Canon Law, and statutes. The original
United States of America were free after the Revolution to have
whatever laws they chose, and some voices strongly advocated
Civil Law systems to represent a rationalistic republicanism and
a clean break from the colonial past. But the legal traditions of
Westminster were too strong to allow much of a departure,
especially since they had been embodied in a systematic study,
written in English and designed as a textbook for beginners,
Blackstone's *Commentaries on the Laws of England.* Canada remained politically subject to Parliament and legally under the
tutelage of the British courts for another century, but the divergent
political lives of Canada and the States have not resulted in any
notable breakup of their shared legal culture and language.

Suggested Reading

Lawrence M. Friedman, *A History of American Law* (2d ed.;
New York: Simon and Schuster, 1986) is a definitive model history,
thorough and well documented, beginning with the colonial period.
John Henry Merriman, *The Civil Law Tradition: An Introduction
to the Legal Systems of Western Europe and Latin America* (Stanford, California: Stanford University Press, 1969) is a clear summary of history and substance.

Terminology

This list consists of legal Americanisms.

ambulance chaser The old European ambulances were either hospital carts following an army or sedan chairs to carry the indigent sick to hospitals. **Ambulance chaser**, meaning a liability lawyer in quest of contingency fees, is an American coinage.

a Blackstone a lawyer with one book.

boilerplate [E] the standard legal verbiage, as used in real estate and other documents. In the mid-19th century the word was newspaper slang for a stereotype plate, a printing block for one or more columns of advertising or political electioneering, cast as a single piece and offered to newspapers for insertion in their news columns.

highgrading California miners' slang for theft, based on panning or digging upgrade from a valid stream claim.

hoosegow Western U.S. spelling of the Spanish *juzgado*, a judicial prison.

hornbook law a mid-19th-century phrase meaning basic law, as learned from commonly available books such as Blackstone, Espinasse's *Nisi Prius* or Peake's *Evidence*. A hornbook consisted of an alphabet and perhaps a Psalm, printed to serve as a reading primer on one sheet of paper, which was covered with a sheet of shaved horn to keep it clean while the infant scholar traced the letters.

horseshedding a witness The early American circuits were often served by only two rudimentary buildings at any given stop, the courthouse (doubling if necessary as a tavern) and the horse shed. A lawyer would have use the latter for privacy to prepare and coach the witnesses he had never met before.

lynch "to hang after summary trial", named after a revolutionary-era partisan terrorist Captain Lynch of Virginia, who did it to Loyalists.

a nisi prius lawyer one without theoretical grounding, but ready to work in civil cases as in a court of *nisi prius,* and likely an owner of Isaac Espinasse's famous book *A Digest of the Law of Actions at Nisi Prius* (London, 1789 and later editions; Philadelphia, 1792). "Espinasse's Nisi Prius" was one of the saddlebag books of the frontier circuit lawyers, until its bad English reputation (for which see Mathew, p. 368) caught up with it.

palimony a recent coinage, based on **alimony** (q.v. in chapter 11) and the Marvin case, where the plaintiff's expectations were not based on contract or sacrament, but only on friendship, and a fragile one at that.

posse [L] short for *posse comitatus*, "the might of the county", which the Old English sheriff or constable could call out and command in case of a general disturbance.

racket When created in England, this word meant a noisy disturbance; the American slang usage (from the 20's) meant a complex of criminal activities always including a pattern of extortion. The word and its offspring **racketeering** are used even in official documents to refer to this large and vague idea.

shotgun charge or **Allen charge** A judge's charge to a jury that they should be agreeable, indicating that he intends to keep them until they reach a verdict. The proper name comes from Allen v. U.S., 164 U.S. 492.

shyster a lawyer who shyly hides from publicity.

squatter's rights the right of occupiers of land without legal title, possibly a humorous translation of the German *Besitz*.

Chapter Twenty

Logical Argument and Evidence

Logic is the technique of building knowledge by deriving valid inferences from true premises. Our western tradition of formal logic stretches back continuously as far as our legal history does, but to Athens rather than to Rome. It was Aristotle, writing and lecturing in Athens late in the 5th century BC, who systematized the method of securing true propositions by the critical assembly of words, and of proceeding from truth to truth in formally constructed arguments called syllogisms.

For illustration, here is a classical syllogism, this one a deductive syllogism:

ALL MEN ARE MORTAL	(major premise, axiom, maxim)
SOCRATES IS A MAN	(minor premise, particular application, *factum probans*)
SOCRATES IS MORTAL	(conclusion, *factum probandum*)

Throughout the middle ages, the technique of Aristotelian logic, translated into Latin, was a part of all higher education, one of the Seven Liberal Arts that led to the degrees of Bachelor of Arts and Master of Arts. Logic was therefore a prerequisite for graduate study in Civil and Canon Law, and the university lecturers in the law frequently used this "scholastic" logic in their writing, case demonstrations, and debates because it was such a useful tool and because any educated person could be presumed to know it. The technique of logic and its terminology also seeped into the courts and discussions of English Common Law, and it is still to be found scattered through legal discourse, especially in discussions of the truth and reliability of evidence and the process of deriving valid inferences from it.

Terminology

academic question [HLE] Academe was a sacred olive grove near Athens in which the philosopher Plato held his school; so any school of free, particularly idealistic discussion can be called an academy, and a question that is suitable for speculative debate rather than for adjudication is called an academic one; roughly equivalent to **moot**, q.v. above in chapter 10.

a contrario sensu [L] "[arguing] from the opposite direction"; on the other hand.

a fortiori [L] "from a stronger [cause]", all the more so; e.g. the presumption of innocence must be respected in misdemeanor cases, and *a fortiori* in capital murder.

a posteriori [L] [argument] from observed particulars to a general judgement; inductive reasoning or experimental research.

a priori [L] [argument] from a general principle to a particular instance; deductive.

adduce [LE] "to bring [evidence] to" an argument.

ad hominem [L] an argument pointed "at the person", intended to persuade by reference to the adversary's bad character.

ad infinitum [L] "to infinity", a short way of naming an unlimited progression.

ad rem [L] an argument directed "to the matter" at hand.

affidavit [LE] "he swore in faith", used as a noun for a voluntary declaration on oath, written and signed. The maker is called the **affiant**.

ambiguity [LFE] "leading both ways", doubleness of meaning.

analogy [HLE] "reasoning back again (Greek *ana + logos*)", the argument that like causes have like results and *vice versa.*

animus [L] "mind", "intention". The ablative *animo* ... means "with the intention ..."

ante litem motam [L] "before the lawsuit was started", characterizing something that was done or said when the doer or sayer was disinterested, i.e. had no motive for deception.

arguendo [L] "for the sake of argument", proposed only hypothetically.

aver [LFE] from the Latin *verum,* "true"; to assert as true. The noun is **averment**.

axiom [HE] from the Greek for "worthy": a proposition that is worthy of belief, undenied, regarded as self-evident. Axioms serve well as major premises or **maxims**.

begging the question [L>E] from the Latin *petitio probandi*, the offering of the very proposition that is to be proven, as evidence in the proof: a circular argument.

bias [FE] From the Middle French *biais*, "slant"; a leaning away from objective truth toward one side of a dispute.

burden of proof [L>E] translated from the Latin *onus probandi*. Whichever side a **presumption** favors, the other side has the burden of proving the contrary.

circular argument [LE] a formal argument, such as a syllogism, that illegitimately introduces the conclusion as a part of the proof.

circumstantial evidence [LE] evidence consisting of facts that are associated with the matter to be proven, as contrasted with the direct testimony of witnesses.

color [LE] "appearance" and so also pretense.

corroborate [LE] to strengthen, support; *robur* is the Latin word for oak wood.

cui bono [L] "Whom does it benefit?" a short form of the argument that interest is a motive to crime or conspiracy. The Latin formula is a correct (if unusual) double dative: "for a good thing, to whom?"

de facto [L] "from a fact", "by an act", the contrary of *de jure*.

de jure [L] "from right", "by the law", legitimate.

demonstrative evidence [LE] visible and tangible evidence, not testimony.

deponent [LE] "one who lays down (*de + ponere*)" a statement; a deposition is a formal entry of evidence.

duress [LFE] from the Latin *durus*, "hard", *duritia*, "hardness", pressure, coercion that limits the freedom of a person's will.

factum probandum [L] "the fact to be proved" (plural *facta probanda*), the conclusion of an argument, in contrast to *factum probans*, "a proving fact" (plural *facta probantia*), which is part of the evidence.

Falsus in uno, falsus in omnibus. [L] "False in one thing, false in all." The presumption against the whole testimony of a witness who has once lied, or one who has been convicted of a *crimen falsi*, q.v. in chapter 12 above.

germane [LE] The Latin *germanus* means a relative, especially a sibling or first cousin; **germane** means related to the matter at issue.

hearsay [GE] a mock-ignorant expression for unacceptable evidence consisting of the secondary witness of words. A *locus classicus* for the exclusion of hearsay occurs three quarters of the way through chapter 34 of Dickens' *Pickwick Papers*, in the breach of promise case Bardell v. Pickwick:

> "Oh, quite enough to get, sir, as the soldier said ven [sic] they ordered him three hundred and fifty lashes," replied Sam.
> "You must not tell us what the soldier, or any other man, said, sir," interposed the judge; "it's not evidence."

hostile [LE] from the Latin *hostis,* "enemy"; "inimical", favoring the adversary. A hostile witness may be cross-examined, even by the side that called the witness.

infer [LE] "carry in [to understanding]": to derive a conclusion logically from evidence. To **imply** or "fold in" means to hint at something without overtly stating it; one's hearer may then **infer** it from the hint.

ipso facto [L] "by the fact itself", without further process. For example, the signing of a will before witnesses makes a valid will *ipso facto*, without registration or deposit.

leading question [GE,LE] one which contains indication of how the questioner wants it answered; such questions are considered objectionable on direct examination.

moral certainty [L>E] practical certainty, short of absolute assurance, based on habitual behavior (*mores*). The phrase does *not* imply that the one holding it is a moral person who is not to be blamed in case of error.

mutatis mutandis [L] "with those things changed that should be changed", "with the necessary modifications". For example, a contract of lease of a horse and wagon will serve, *mutatis mutandis*, for the lease of a truck.

nemine contradicente, nem. con. [L] "with no one speaking against ". This phrase characterizes a decision of an official body with no negative votes, even if not unanimous. It also expresses the logical *argumentum ex silentio*, the "argument from silence": if a report is published in a reputable journal to the effect that a certain legislator is on the payroll of a certain corporation, and the shocking allegation is not denied, then it is reasonable, *nemine contradicente*, to believe it.

non sequitur [L] "It does not follow", the logical criticism that a particular conclusion is not validly derived from the stated premises. Usually used in English as a noun phrase:

"Your client is unemployed: he is unwilling to make an honest living."
"That is a non sequitur. The fact that he is unemployed is no reason to suppose that he is dishonest, or does not want a steady job."

opinion evidence [LE] evidence of what the witness infers or believes; usually it is only permitted from expert witnesses in the fields of their expertise.

parol [HLFE] "oral", not written, an adjective used with the nouns **evidence, contract, promise,** etc. This is one of several dozen fascinating derivatives from the Greek *parabola*, "something tossed alongside"; this was the word for a comparison or exemplary story (hence **parable**) and for a conversation back and forth, cf. **parole** above in chapter 9. **Oral** comes from the Latin *os,* "mouth".

per se [L] "by himself/herself/themselves", "in itself", "as such", "taken alone".

prejudice [LE] "judgement in advance" of evidence: bias, deprivation of the right to be impartially heard.

presumption [LE] "assumption in advance [of evidence]": an instrument for the process of proving or disproving. Unlike **prejudice, presumption** is not final. A presumption, e.g. the presumption of innocence, or the presumption in favor of the one in possession, lays the **burden of proof** on the other party.

prima facie [L] "at first appearance", "presumably". A *prima facie* case is a sufficient argument and evidence by the plaintiff or prosecutor to stand unless overcome by the defendant. It discharges and transfers the burden of proof.

privileged communications [LE] exchanges of confidential information that enjoy legal protection from forced disclosure; such are conversations between husband and wife, priest and penitent, lawyer and client, doctor and patient.

purport [LFE] "bearing (Latin *portus*)": the meaning of a document, or the relevance of a piece of evidence.

real evidence [LE] things as evidence.

reductio ad absurdum [L] "reduction to the absurd", a defense in debate which consists of drawing the most extreme and ridiculous conclusions from the opponent's premises or a twisted version of them.

relevancy [LE] the condition of bearing on or relating to the matter under discussion or the issue in court. The form **relevance** means the same.

res gestae [L] "things done", acts (singular *res gesta*). One answer to the objection against **hearsay** is the argument that some words are really acts, *res gestae*, because they are directly associated with acts, e.g. "Take that, you hound!" or "You've killed me, honey!"

Res inter alios acta, alteri nocere non debet. [L] "A thing done between others should not harm a third party." Broom (pp. 954-967) explores the application of this maxim to the law of evidence, and finds a treasury of exceptions.

scintilla of evidence [LE] "spark", the smallest visible illumination.

secondary evidence [LE] evidence of evidence, for example oral testimony about the contents of a lost document.

seriatim [L] "one after another", individually.

situs [L] "place" as a legal characteristic.

straw man [L>GE] a fake person or interest. The phrase is used to signify a merely nominal party or beneficiary, a "front". It can also mean your adversary's restatement of your position, so weak and flawed that he can easily push it over.

sui generis [L] "of its own genus", not belonging to a larger class, and so not subject to more general rules.

tangible [LE] "touchable", perceptible, not only a matter of opinion.

time immemorial [L>E] from the Latin *memoria*, "memory"; a time before records. A custom or usage "from time immemorial" is one that is older than any contrary testimony. **Time out of mind** is a similar idea, but limited in extent to the memory of persons now living.

Chapter Twenty-One

Torts

All our substantive law can be divided into three grand categories: crime, contracts, and torts. To put it another way, torts are all the civil cases that do not arise from contracts. The word itself is from French, and means a "twist", a distortion of relations between persons' rights, a civil wrong. The Roman Civil Law word **delictum** covered both **crime** and **tort**, and must now be translated as one or the other of these very different categories. Governments in the 20th century have expanded their powers in several ways, one being the extension of criminal jurisdiction into areas once covered by tort law. For example, where once the neighbor of a barking dog might bring a civil suit to abate a nuisance, he will often now call the police to issue a citation under a local noise ordinance.

Res ipsa loquitur, so often used in cases of liability by negligence that it is abbreviated *r.i.l.*, deserves special attention. Here is a unique case of Latin terminology that became internationally current in the law only in the last century. A pedestrian named Byrne, walking by a warehouse owned by one Boadle in Scotland Road, Liverpool, was struck down and seriously injured by a barrel of flour that fell from an upper window. Byrne sued in the Liverpool Court of Passage, but, because he brought no proof of any negligence by Boadle or his agents, he was nonsuited by the presiding Assessor. He petitioned the Exchequer for a rule *nisi*, and the case came there on 25 November 1863. Chief Baron Pollock observed, "There are certain cases of which it may be said res ipsa loquitur, and this seems one of them. In some cases the Courts have held that the mere fact of the accident having occurred is evidence of negligence, as, for instance, in the case of railway collisions." Those words did not occur in the unanimous holding of the court, but in the Chief Baron's interruption of Charles Russell's argument showing cause for the defendant, and they would have been lost but for the rather full account in Hurlstone and Coltman, *The Exchequer Reports* 2 (1864) 722-729. Lawyers of the United Kingdom, Canada and the United States, eager for this particular precedent, adopted it in its Latin words, and have used them subsequently as if they were a maxim.

Terminology

abate [LFE] "to beat down", "destroy". The noun **abatement** is generally milder: "reduction", e.g. of rent or of a nuisance. The French *abbatre* came from the Latin *battuere*, itself apparently picked up from a Gallic word meaning the same thing, "to pound". **Battery**, below, is a cognate.

abuse [LE] "to use wrongly" or "a wrong use"; a repeated action that is not good usage or custom.

accident [LE] "a falling to (*ad + cadere*)", "befalling", a misfortune. The original Latin referred to a lot falling out of a jar, or dice from a cup, emphasizing the fact that the event is unexpected.

actio damni injuria [L] "action of loss by injury", the general class name for actions for damages in Civil Law, adopted in English Law. To be sustained, there must be both real loss and real wrong; cf. *damnum absque injuria* below.

actio ex delicto [L] "action derived from a tort", e.g. nuisance, malpractice, etc.

action on the case [LE] a clumsy adaptation of the law of actions in **trespass** to new uses, especially **negligence**. See the historical explanation in Plucknett, pp. 468-472.

act of God an accident entirely without human agency, and not actionable.

assault [LFE] from the Latin *ad* + *saltare*, "to jump at"; a physical attack on a person, even before it reaches its mark: attempted battery.

battery [LFE] "a beating", now usually criminal rather than tortious. **Abate**, above, is cognate.

bona vacantia [L] "vacant goods" (singular *bonum vacans*): without an owner; stray or salvage, for the finder to keep.

colloquium [L] the context or application of words, specifically to a person in regard to whom they are slanderous. For example, the words "He is a well-paid agent of several oil companies", not defamatory in themselves, in colloquium to a Member of Parliament would be slanderous. Colloquium can be achieved by **innuendo**, q.v. below.

contra pacem [L] "against the peace", a phrase in a criminal indictment; also used in complaints of trespass, when the plaintiff was making use of public authority against the defendant.

conversion [LE] "turning around (*con* + *versio*)" another's goods to one's own use, and the action for damages arising from it.

damnum absque injuria [L] "loss without wrong" and so not actionable; neither is *injuria absque damno*.

detinue [LFE] "holding (Latin *tentus*, French *tenue*) away", "keeping", a Common Law action for the recovery of goods in kind, without a need to prove criminal theft.

duty [LFE] "what is owed (Latin *debitum*, French *du*)", the reciprocal of law and of right. See Fullager, pp. 2-6 for an eloquently expressed worry over this excessively general and much misused term.

ex delicto [L] "from wrong", "from tort", the whole class of private actions that are not *ex contractu*.

ferae naturae [L] "of wild nature", e.g. a fox, even if kept as a pet, is not a domestic (*domitae naturae*) animal.

Injuria non excusat injuriam. [L] "Wrong does not excuse wrong".

injury [LE] "wrong", used popularly as if it meant harm, especially bodily harm.

innuendo [L] "by nodding at (*in* + *nuere*)", "with a nod", the word in a charge of slander that introduced the explanation of why the words quoted were defamatory against the plaintiff in particular, e.g. "The defendant said 'Some people just have no morals', with the **innuendo** that Vice-Principal Doe is an amoral person."

In pari delicto melior est conditio possidentis aut defendentis. [L] "In a case of equal wrong, the one in possession, or the defendant, is in a better position." The other party has the burden of proof. Broom, pp. 713-729, discusses one of the several variants of this statement of presumption.

libel [LE] "little book"; the term means specifically a slanderous pamphlet, a defamatory writing; and also the full written plea in *jus commune* and the old initial pleading in Admiralty cases; cf. **bill** above in chapter 17.

malice [LE] "badness", desire to harm.

negligence [LE] "the state of not attending to", the single word most packed with implications in the law of torts. See Fullagar's thoughtful article, pp. 2-6.

nuisance [LFE] The Latin *nocere* means "to harm", and the French equivalent *nuisir* gave the English doublets **annoyance** and **nuisance**, both with serious medieval meanings and trivial modern ones. A **nuisance**, briefly, is a use of one's own property to the damage of another. The specific **attractive nuisance** works by first enticing, then harming, e.g. an outdoor swimming pool.

per quod [L] "by which", the beginning of the clause in an old Common Law writ of trespass that explains the damage caused.

persecution [LE] "a following through (*per* + *secutio*)", the malicious pressing of lawsuits beyond legitimate cause.

proximate cause [LE] "nearest cause", the last in a series of causes of an accidental loss.

quare clausum fregit, qu.cl.fr. [L] "because he broke the enclosure", the clarification of a trespass by the particular damage.

redress [LFE] The Latin *redirigere* meant "to set straight again", and so did the French *redresser*. To **redress** is to adjust or remedy an injustice; also, as a noun, "rectification".

res ipsa loquitur, r.i.l. [L] "The thing speaks for itself." A phrase summarizing the presumption of negligence in certain cases, e.g. of a surgical instrument left in a patient; see the introduction to this chapter.

scienter [L] "knowingly", the part of a complaint which alleges the defendant's foreknowledge of the cause of an injury. The full phrase was *scienter et cum malitia praecognita*, "knowingly and with malice aforethought."

Sic utere tuo ut alienum non laedas. [L] "Use your own thing in such a way as not to harm another's." See Broom pp. 365-395 for a rich unpacking of this statement of nuisance.

slander [LFE] spoken defamation. Derived from the Late Latin *scandalum*, which appeared in the Vulgate Bible meaning "a stumbling-block", something that upsets the good behavior of the righteous; **scandal** is a doublet.

tort [LFE] "twist", a civil wrong. The adjective is **tortious** and the doer is called a **tort-feasor**.

trover [FE] "a finding (*trouver*)", a fictitious claim, the civil parallel of criminal theft: a suit seeking damages, often paired with **conversion**, q.v. above.

vi et armis [L] "by force and arms", a phrase in a trespass writ that justifies the plaintiff's call for public force.

vis major [L] "greater power", rendered in French as *force majeur*, a natural cause, stronger than due diligence; an act of God.

Volenti non fit injuria. [L] "No wrong is done to one consenting." *Digest* rule 145, *Sextus* rule 27, and see Broom, pp. 268-277: "No one can maintain an action for a wrong when he has consented to the act which occasions his loss." This consent is often called today "assumption of risk".

Chapter Twenty-Two

Corporation, Partnership, and Securities

The legal concept of corporation was one of the cleverest crea-
tions of the Roman Civil Law, though the Roman lawyers called
it *societas* or *universitas* (and the latter term has been specialized
to mean a familiar form of scholastic corporation). Under this legal
fiction a number of persons could carry on a necessary work in
a stable manner over generations and through any number of
changes of personnel, using the legal identity of one "person", the
Corporation. The Christian Church organized itself in the Roman
world as a network of corporations, and then preserved the memory
of the Roman Civil Law largely because no other system
understood corporation and could guarantee the churches their
corporate privileges and advantages.

Late in the Middle Ages, the Italian trading companies picked
up the concept of corporation and used it with great creativity to
assemble capital for long-term development and for short ventures.
They invented the *società anonima* or limited-liability company,
the modern form of business corporation, which owns and uses
the money pooled by the shareholders, hires a board of directors,
and makes more money or else goes broke without risking any
more of the owners' wealth than they invested in it.

The late 19th century, especially in America, saw a rapid growth of corporations and many new developments in corporate activities. The courts, using the machinery of equity, acted inventively to prevent the worst abuses of corporate power, and a good deal of the terminology in this area is American English.

Terminology

acid test an Americanism for the **quick asset ratio** of accounting: current assets minus inventory, divided by current liabilities. The same simile, based on the use of nitric or sulfuric acid to test for gold, is applied to any test that is quick, brutal and sure.

blue sky laws State laws governing the sale of securities in airy ventures.

bond [GE] "a tie", either an instrument of indebtedness or security for performance or court appearance.

capital [LE] "of the head": personal, movable property including cash, as opposed to real property. Also, in the old Italian accountry of venture corporations, the total investment appeared as the headline of the account sheet.

company [LIE] from the Latin *com + panis*, Italian *compagnia*, "eating bread together". The medieval Italian trading and banking houses were organized as extended families, complete with dependents who shared a common table with the blood relations of the *padrone*.

corporation [LE] from the Latin *corpus*, "body"; "embodiment", a fictitious legal person vested with the share capital pooled by the owners and having their zeal for profit as its soul.

debenture [LE] a consecrated misspelling of *debentur*, "these things are owed", the beginning word of a promissory note from a corporation, now especially an unsecured one.

defalcation [LE] The Latin *falx* meant "sickle", and the expression *falcem in segetem alienam mittere*, "to put one's sickle into another's harvest" meant embezzlement.

delegate [LE] "to send a personal messenger"; or as a noun, "a messenger (*legatus*)", an agent for a particular negotiation.

dividend [LE] "the thing to be divided (*dividendum*)", a profit distributable among the shareholders of a corporation.

limited [LE] "having a boundary set"; specifically, **limited liability** is the risk of corporate loss, which can go no further for each shareholder than the cost of his shares.

merger [LFE] "drowning [in another corporation] (Latin *mergere*)", one of the only ways that a corporation can die. The other is dissolution.

monopoly [HLE] "belonging to one city or market (Greek *mono + polis*)", the exclusive control by one seller of the sale of a particular commodity.

option [LE] "choice", a right to buy stock in a company ahead of the general public.

partner [LFE] from the Latin *portionarius*, "one entitled to a share", transformed in French into *part-teneur*, "holder of a part".

pierce the corporate veil [LFE] a little fragment of poetry from American business law. The **veil** is the corporation's legal identity, masking the directors and owners and rendering them immune, as individuals, for their acts in pursuit of the purposes of the corporation. When the veil has been used to cover illegal activities, the court can pierce it and see them as individuals.

power of attorney [LFE] an instrument empowering another to act legally in one's place; cf. proxy below.

preferred stock [LE,GE] shares of ownership of a corporation with priority before common stock for payment, both of dividends and of capital in case of dissolution.

pro rata [L] The full phrase was *pro rata parte,* "according to the agreed proportion".

proxy [LFE] The Latin *procurator*, "caretaker", is roughly the [FE] **attorney**, a legal representative; and [L] *procuratio*, [FE] **proxy** is a power of attorney, most frequently used for corporate voting by representation. A **proctor** who oversees a university examination does so as the faculty's representative.

scope of authority [HE,LE] "range or angle of [delegated] authority", what the officers of a corporation can do as such, under the **corporate veil**.

securities [LE] from the Latin *se + cura*, "free of care"; "safeties", instruments of debts receivable from corporations, and instruments of ownership of corporations: bonds and stocks, respectively.

share [GE] "slice", a piece of corporate ownership.

subscription [LE] "a writing under (*sub + scribere*)" or "underwriting", a list of persons who have contracted to buy stock, also their contract to do so. This is a process of assembling capital for a new venture; the corporation does not come into existence, or expand its capitalization, until the subscription list is full.

ultra vires [L] "beyond its powers", excessive to a corporation's charter.

vested [LE] "robed": a right or power actually owned by a person is **vested in** that person; one who is actually able to use such a right or power is **vested with** it.

Chapter Twenty-Three

Sovereignty and Conflict of Laws

This chapter is concerned with some of the technical language that is used in describing the legal relations of states to their citizens and to each other. Taxation figures in this list, and so do constitutional law and the complex of questions called Conflict of Laws.

Terminology

abjuration [LE] "swearing off", renunciation by oath.

ad valorem [L] a tax rated "to the value" of the property taxed; the alternative is a **specific** tax such as a poll tax or license fee.

assess [LE] "to sit beside (*ad + sedere*)", to advise a judge, especially in points of law or technical matters, as an **assessor** does; so, specifically, to evaluate property for fiscal purposes, an expert function that once had the name **taxation** (see **tax** below).

ballot [LIE] "little ball", a counter used for voting, as in **blackball**; the word bullet, sometimes paired with this one for contrast, is in fact a doublet; both come from the Latin *bulla*, a round lead seal.

barratry [FE] The Middle French *barater* meant "to exchange", "to switch". Possibly under suggestion from the word **bar** it has come to mean the marketing of justice by a judge or prosecutor, or their stirring up litigation for their profit; also, in Admiralty, the fraudulent switching of cargo by a ship's master and crew.

breach of the peace In this phrase, **peace** is the condition of order that is part of a sovereign's dignity and honor and the wealth of a country or town. The area within sight of a French town's walls, within which the town forbade and would punish violence, used to be called its *paix* or peace. Disorderly behavior that lay outside the scope of crime (murder and robbery) was tried, in England, by local magistrates called **justices of the peace**.

bylaw [NE] from the Old Norse, "village law".

condemnation [LE] a sentence of "complete loss (*con* + *damnum*)", a capital sentence with seizure of the felon's property by the court; more recently equivalent to **expropriation**, q.v. below.

confiscation [LE] "complete seizure for the fisc". *Fiscus*, "a money bag" was the name for the Roman emperors' financial office, kept separate from the public treasury; the same idea reappears in England in the Privy Purse.

conflict of interest [LE] refers to any kind of clash between an official's duty to serve the public advantage and his own benefit.

conflict of laws [LE,NE] a branch of jurisprudence that sorts out the problems that arise when different legal systems overlap on one person, case, question, property, etc. Various ways the law can be identified as applicable are summed up in the phrases *lex* ... below, q.v.

constitution [LE] from the Latin *con* + *statutum*, "establishment", and so a law laid down by a prince such as an emperor or pope; or the structure of a state and the law that describes and governs that structure: the **organic law**, q.v. below.

contempt of court [LE] an attack on the dignity and effectiveness of a court, which the judge may punish without trial, in the last surviving relic of royal summary justice.

corruption [LE] "total breakdown", especially of public duty by bribe-taking.

court martial [LFE] a military court, a relic of the privileged, extra-legal status of the medieval military caste, the knights; and also of the summary judgement without appeal which Roman military commanders exercised on campaign. As part of a civil emergency, normal legal rights are sometimes suspended and the general population subjected to the controls of martial law.

election [LE] "choice", not necessarily by the votes of all concerned.

eminent domain [LFE] "overshadowing (*eminens*) lordship", such as a sovereignty has over all the land; power of **expropriation**, q.v. below.

excise [LE] "cutting out (*ex + cisio*)", a tax on movables in trade that once consisted of taking a share in kind as the goods passed a port.

ex post facto [L] "after the fact", "retroactive", describing, e.g., a law to punish a particular past act as a crime, prohibited by the U. S. Constitution (1.10).

expropriation [LE] "removal from private (*proprium*) ownership".

extradition [LE] from the Latin *ex + trans + dare*, "a handing over outside", surrender of a prisoner by one jurisdiction to another.

immunity [LE] "[right of] non-payment", a **privilege** (q.v. below) of exemption from a public burden.

impeach [LFE] "to put guilt (Latin *peccatum*, French *péché*) upon", to charge a public official with crime.

inauguration [LE] "a beginning by taking the auguries". Roman public enterprises began by a fortune-telling examination of the entrails of the sacrificial animals.

jurisdiction [LE] "declaration of the law", the power of legislation and judicial sentence.

lese majesty [LFE] "a wound (Latin *laesa*, French *lèse*) to the majesty", the Civil Law crime that was the original crime in England, any form of treason or injury to the king's power.

lex domicilii [L] "law of the domicile" of the defendant.

lex fori [L] "law of the court" hearing the case.

lex loci contractus [L] "law of the place of the contract".

lex loci delicti [L] "law of the place of the crime (or tort)".

lex loci rei sitae [L] "law of the place where the thing is located".

malfeasance [LFE] from the Latin *mala* + *factio*, French *faisance*, "bad performance" of a public function.

Nemo debet esse judex in propria sua causa. [L] "No one ought to be judge in his own cause", an expression of *Digest* 3.5.1, applied severely against conflicts of interest in Broom, pp. 116-121.

Nemo de domo sua extrahi debet. [L] "No one should be dragged from his own house", *Digest* rule 103. For the Civil Law, a Roman's home was his temple, the shrine of his ancestral gods. Coke L.C.J. expressed the English rule in a famous phrase, repeated by Blackstone and recently quoted by Senator Talmadge in the Watergate hearings as hornbook law: "Every man's house is his castle; even though the winds of heaven may blow through it, the King of England cannot enter it."

nepotism [LE] "nephewism". The choice of this word for the bad practice of favoring relatives with public benefits, especially employments, shows that it was prevalent among the medieval clergy, because they seldom had legitimate sons to promote, only nephews, *nepotes*.

organic law [HLE,NE] the law, often called a constitution, which regulates the relations and operations of the various bodies, functions, and interests (the organs or instruments) of a state.

poll [GE] "crown of the head", and so "the counting of heads" in a plebiscite or popular election in general; or a specific tax of a population "per head".

prerogative [LE] from the Latin *prae* + *rogatus*, "appointed to lead"; "the pre-eminence" of sovereign authority, and an adjective applied to several English writs which mobilized that power, notably *Certiorari* (see chapter 13), *Mandamus* (see chapter 6), *Habeas corpus* (see chapter 12), *Quo warranto* (below in this chapter), and also the obsolete *Procedendo* and *Prohibition*.

privilege [L] from *privilegium*, "a private law", a special exemption or concession to a class or group of persons; the internal law of a franchise such as the military, the clergy, a convent, or a ghetto.

pro tanto [L] "for that much", compensation for an expropriation without prejudice to a claim for more.

quo warranto [L] "by what warrant?", the name of a prerogative writ questioning the legitimacy of a court, a tax-collection, or other exercise of public power.

quorum [LE] An official body has a number of members "of whom" a portion can conduct its business with legal effect.

referendum [LE] "a thing to be carried back" to the citizen body by its representatives.

Riot Act an English statute of 1715 providing criminal penalties for any assembly which did not disperse when the Act itself was read; so "reading the riot act" in ordinary usage means a peremptory assertion of authority against disorder.

sanction [LE] "a making sacred", a confirmation or enforcement of a law by the highest authority, taken to be divine.

sinecure [LE] "without care", originally a church position without the "cure of souls", i.e. pastoral care; now any position, especially a public one, with a stipend but no important duties.

sovereign [LFE] from the Latin *supremus*, through the French *souverain*, "supreme"; the highest level of political authority.

Star Chamber [LE] a room in Westminster Palace with gold-leaf stars on its dark blue ceiling, where the royal Council met as a prerogative court of law beginning in the 13th century. Its secret, summary procedure gave it a bad reputation in the reigns of the first Stuart kings, James I and Charles I, in the early 17th century.

tax [LE] from the frequentative of the Latin *tangere*, "to touch"; "to feel over", to estimate; later, to assign a fiscal value; finally, to collect fiscal levies.

treason [LFE] from the Latin *traditio*, through the French *trahison*, "handing over" a guest or a trust to an enemy.

vote [LE] The Latin noun *votum* meant "wish" and also "vow".

warrant [GFE] from the Old High German *werento*, "protection", authoritative support, and a document that grants it to an agent of the authority, e.g. for a search or arrest.

References

Alderman, Sidney S. "The French Language in English and American Law", *Canadian Bar Review* 28 (1950) 1104-1123.

Ballentine, James A. *Law Dictionary with Pronunciations.* (2d ed. Rochester, N.Y., 1948).

Black, Henry Campbell. *Black's Law Dictionary*: Definitions of the Terms and Phrases of American and English Jurisprudence, Ancient and Modern. (1st ed. 1891; 5th ed., St. Paul, Minnesota, 1979).

Blackstone, William. *Commentaries on the Laws of England.* (1765-1769 and many later editions).

Broom, Herbert. *A Selection of Legal Maxims, Classified and Illustrated.* (7th American, from the 5th London edition; Philadelphia, 1874).

Chitty, Joseph. *A Treatise on Pleading, and Parties to Actions.* (1808; 9th American from 6th London ed., 1844)

The Civil Law. English translation by S.P. Scott. (17 vols.; Cincinnati, 1932; reprint New York, 1973). Almost entirely devoted to the Corpus Juris Civilis of Justinian; the Digest occupies vols. 2-11, and the Rules of Law are in vol. 11, pp. 297-318.

Engelmann, Arthur et al., eds. *History of Continental Civil Procedure.* Trans. Robert W. Millar. Continental Legal History 7. (New York, 1927; reprint 1969).

Espinasse, Isaac. *A Digest of the Law of Actions at Nisi Prius.* (London, 1789 and later editions; Philadelphia, 1792).

Friedman, Lawrence M. *A History of American Law.* (2d ed.; New York, 1986).

Fullagar, Wilfred K. "Legal Terminology", *Melbourne University Law Review* 1 (1957) 1-8.

Grimm, Jacob. "Von der Poesie im Recht", *Zeitschrift für geschichtliche Rechtswissenschaft* 2 (1816) 25-99; reprinted in his *Kleinere Schriften* (Hildeshiem, 1965) vol. 6, 152-191.

Heath, Shirley Brice. "The Context of Professional Languages: an Historical Overview" in *Language in Public Life*, ed. James E. Alatis and G. Richard Tucker (Washington, 1979), pp. 102-118.

Holdsworth, William Searle. *Charles Dickens as a Legal Historian.* (New Haven, 1928).

Hunnisett, R.F. *The Medieval Coroner.* (Cambridge, 1961).

Jolowicz, H.F. *Roman Foundations of Modern Law.* (Oxford, 1957).

Kent, James. *Commentaries on American Law.* (4 vols.; New York, 1826-1830, reprinted 1971).

Laskin, Bora. *The British Tradition in Canadian Law.* (London, 1969).

Maitland, Frederick William. *The Forms of Action at Common Law.* (Cambridge, 1936; reprinted 1954).

Mathew, Theobald. "Law-French", *Law Quarterly Review* 54 (1938) 358-369.

Mellinkoff, David. *The Language of the Law.* (Boston and Toronto, 1963).

Merryman, John Henry. *The Civil Law Tradition*: An Introduction to the Legal Systems of Western Europe and Latin America. (Stanford, 1969).

Millar, Robert Wyness. "The Lineage of Some Procedural Words", *American Bar Association Journal* 25 (1939) 1023-1029.

O'Barr, William M. "The Language of the Law" in *Language in the USA*, ed. Charles A. Ferguson and Shirley Brice Heath (New York, 1981) pp. 386-406.

Oxford English Dictionary. Ed. James A.H. Murray et al. (12 vols.; Oxford, 1933).

Oxford Latin Dictionary. Ed. P.G.W. Glare. (Oxford, 1982).

Peake, Thomas. *A Compendium of the Law of Evidence.* (London, 1801; Philadelphia, 1802).

Plucknett, Theodore F.T. *A Concise History of the Common Law.* (5th ed.; Boston, 1956).

Rembar, Charles. *The Law of the Land.* (New York, 1980).

Smith, Thomas B. *Scotland: the Development of its Laws and Constitution.* (London, 1962).

Stein, Peter. *Regulae juris: from Juristic Rules to Legal Maxims.* (Edinburgh, 1966).

Vinogradoff, Paul. *Roman Law in Medieval Europe.* (2d ed. Oxford, 1929, repr. London, 1968).

Warren, W.L. *Henry II.* (Berkeley, 1973).

Weihofen, Henry. *Legal Writing Style.* (St. Paul, 1961).

Index

Note: The index of Maxims is on page 160.

mistrial 104
mitigating circumstances 77
modus operandi 104
moiety 71
monopoly 139
moot 66
moral certainty 127
mortgage 97
mortmain 97
motion 23
murder 77
mutatis mutandis 127
mutual 116
natural law 110
ne exeat 23
negligence 135
negotiable instrument 116
nemine contradicente 128
nepotism 146
next friend 71
nisi 72
nisi prius 91
nisi prius lawyer 122
nolle prosequi, nol.pros. 23
nolo contendere 104
nominal 47
non est factum 39
non obstante veredicto 47
non sequitur 128
nonsuit 23
notary public 83
novation 39
nudum pactum 39
nuisance 135
nulla bona 39
nunc pro tunc 47
nuncupative 58
oath 67
obiter dictum 45
objection 23
of course 24
of record 83
on all fours 111
operative words 39
opinion evidence 128
option 139
ordeal 100
organic law 146
outlaw 61

oyer and terminer 67
oyez 67
palimony 122
pardon 61
parens patriae 72
pari passu 39
parol 128
parole 61
partial, partiality 47
particeps criminis 77
partner 139
party 40
patent 83
peers 47
penitentiary 62
peppercorn 40
per capita 58
per curiam 47
per quod 135
per se 128
per stirpes 58
peremptory 53
perpetuity 58
persecution 135
persona 40
personalty 98
petit jury 91
petition 24
pierce the corporate veil 139
plagiarism 77
plaintiff 24
plat 98
pleading 24
plebiscite 32
police 77
poll 146
posse 122
post mortem 104
power of attorney 140
praecipe 91
preferred stock 140
prejudice 128
premises 98
prerogative 146
prescription 98
presentment 104
presents 84
presumption 128
prima facie 128

Maxims

Aequitas sequitur legem. 107
Aliud est celare, aliud tacere. 35
Audi alteram partem. 20
Caveat emptor. 114
De minimis non curat lex. 21
Ex dolo malo non oritur actio. 37
Ex nudo pacto non oritur actio. 37
Ex turpi causa non oritur actio. 38
Expressio unius est exclusio alterius. 109
Falsus in uno, falsus in omnibus. 126
Id certum est quod certum reddi potest. 109
Ignorantia facti excusat; ignorantia juris non excusat. 103
Impossibilium nulla obligatio est. 110
In pari delicto melior est conditio possidentis aut defendentis. 134
Injuria non excusat injuriam. 134
Interest reipublicae ut sit finis litium. 46
Mobilia sequuntur personam. 57
Modus et conventio vincunt legem. 39
Nemo de domo sua extrahi debet. 145
Nemo debet esse judex in propria sua causa. 145
Nemo potest plus juris ad alium transferre quam ipse habet. 98
Non videntur qui errant consentire. 110
Noscitur a sociis. 110
Omnis definitio in jure civili periculosa est. 111
Pater is est quem nuptiae demonstrant. 72
Pendente lite nihil innovetur. 24
Qui facit per alium facit per se. 40
Qui prior est tempore, potior est jure. 98
Qui sentit commodum sentire debet et onus. 40
Qui tacet consentire videtur. 77
Quod ab initio non valet, tractu temporis non convalescit. 111
Res inter alios acta, alteri nocere non debet. 129
Res judicata pro veritate accipitur. 48
Respondeat superior. 117
Sic utere tuo ut alienum non laedas. 136
Simplex commendatio non obligat. 117
Stare decisis et non quieta movere. 48
Ubi jus, ibi remedium. 92
Vigilantibus et non dormientibus jura subveniunt. 112
Volenti non fit injuria. 136